DISEASES OF MEMORY

THE INTERNATIONAL SCIENTIFIC SERIES

DISEASES OF MEMORY

AN ESSAY IN THE POSITIVE PSYCHOLOGY

by

TH. RIBOT

TRANSLATED FROM THE FRENCH,

BY WILLIAM HUNTINGTON SMITH

GYAN

Published by

Gyan Publishing House
5, Ansari Road
Daryaganj, New Delhi-110002
Phone: 011-47034999, 9811692060
E-mail: books@gyanbooks.com

Distribution Network
gyanbooks.com
India, USA, Canada, UK, Australia, France

ISBN : 978-81-212-6168-5 (PB)
First Published, 1882

2nd Impression 2021

Printed at: Gyan Press, Delhi.

Diseases of Memory
Author: TH. Ribot

THE

INTERNATIONAL SCIENTIFIC SERIES.

EACH BOOK COMPLETE IN ONE VOLUME, 12MO, AND BOUND IN CLOTH.

I. FORMS OF WATER: a Familiar Exposition of the Origin and Phenomena of Glaciers. By J. TYNDALL, LL. D., F. R. S. With 25 Illustrations. $1.50.

II. PHYSICS AND POLITICS; Or, Thoughts on the Application of the Principles of "Natural Selection" and "Inheritance" to Political Society. By WALTER BAGEHOT. $1.50.

III. FOODS. By EDWARD SMITH, M. D., LL. B., F. R. S. With numerous Illustrations. $1.75.

IV. MIND AND BODY: The Theories of their Relation. By ALEXANDER BAIN, LL. D. With Four Illustrations. $1.50.

V. THE STUDY OF SOCIOLOGY. By HERBERT SPENCER. $1.50.

VI. THE NEW CHEMISTRY. By Professor J. P. COOKE, of Harvard University. With 31 Illustrations. $2.00.

VII. ON THE CONSERVATION OF ENERGY. By BALFOUR STEWART, M. A., LL. D., F. R. S. With 14 Illustrations. $1.50.

VIII. ANIMAL LOCOMOTION; or, Walking, Swimming, and Flying. By J. B. PETTIGREW, M. D., F. R. S., etc. With 130 Illustrations. $1.75.

IX. RESPONSIBILITY IN MENTAL DISEASE. By HENRY MAUDSLEY, M. D. $1.50.

X. THE SCIENCE OF LAW. By Professor SHELDON AMOS. $1.75.

XI. ANIMAL MECHANISM: A Treatise on Terrestrial and Aërial Locomotion. By Professor E. J. MAREY. With 117 Illustrations. $1.75.

XII. THE HISTORY OF THE CONFLICT BETWEEN RELIGION AND SCIENCE. By J. W. DRAPER, M. D., LL. D. $1.75.

XIII. THE DOCTRINE OF DESCENT AND DARWINISM. By Professor OSCAR SCHMIDT (Strasburg University). With 26 Illustrations. $1.50.

XIV. THE CHEMICAL EFFECTS OF LIGHT AND PHOTOGRAPHY. By Dr. HERMANN VOGEL (Polytechnic Academy of Berlin). Translation thoroughly revised. With 100 Illustrations. $2.00.

XV. FUNGI: Their Nature, Influences, Uses, etc. By M. C. COOKE, M. A., LL. D. Edited by the Rev. M. J. BERKELEY, M. A., F. L. S. With 109 Illustrations. $1.50.

XVI. THE LIFE AND GROWTH OF LANGUAGE. By Professor WILLIAM DWIGHT WHITNEY, of Yale College. $1.50.

XVII. MONEY AND THE MECHANISM OF EXCHANGE. By W. STANLEY JEVONS, M. A., F. R. S. $1.75.

XVIII. THE NATURE OF LIGHT, with a General Account of Physical Optics. By Dr. EUGENE LOMMEL. With 188 Illustrations and a Table of Spectra in Chromo-lithography. $2.00.

XIX. ANIMAL PARASITES AND MESSMATES. By Monsieur VAN BENEDEN. With 83 Illustrations. $1.50.

XX. FERMENTATION. By Professor SCHÜTZENBERGER. With 28 Illustrations. $1.50.

XXI. THE FIVE SENSES OF MAN. By Professor BERNSTEIN. With 91 Illustrations. $1.75.

XXII. THE THEORY OF SOUND IN ITS RELATION TO MUSIC. By Professor PIETRO BLASERNA. With numerous Illustrations. $1.50.

New York: D. APPLETON & CO., 1, 3, & 5 Bond Street.

XXIII. STUDIES IN SPECTRUM ANALYSIS. By J. NORMAN LOCKYER, F. R. S. With Six Photographic Illustrations of Spectra, and numerous Engravings on Wood. $2.50.

XXIV. A HISTORY OF THE GROWTH OF THE STEAM-ENGINE. By Professor R. H. THURSTON. With 163 Illustrations. $2.50.

XXV. EDUCATION AS A SCIENCE. By ALEXANDER BAIN, LL. D. $1.75.

XXVI. STUDENTS' TEXT-BOOK OF COLOR, OR, MODERN CHROMATICS. With Applications to Art and Industry. By Professor OGDEN N. ROOD, Columbia College. New edition. With 130 Illustrations. $2.00.

XXVII. THE HUMAN SPECIES. By Professor A. DE QUATREFAGES, Membre de l'Institut. $2.00.

XXVIII. THE CRAYFISH: an Introduction to the Study of Zoölogy. By T. H. HUXLEY, F. R. S. With 82 Illustrations. $1.75.

XXIX. THE ATOMIC THEORY. By Professor A. WURTZ. Translated by E. CLEMINSHAW, F. C. S. $1.50.

XXX. ANIMAL LIFE AS AFFECTED BY THE NATURAL CONDITIONS OF EXISTENCE. By KARL SEMPER. With Two Maps and 106 Woodcuts. $2.00.

XXXI. SIGHT: An Exposition of the Principles of Monocular and Binocular Vision. By JOSEPH LE CONTE, LL. D. With 132 Illustrations. $1.50.

XXXII. GENERAL PHYSIOLOGY OF MUSCLES AND NERVES. By Professor J. ROSENTHAL. With 75 Illustrations. $1.50.

XXXIII. ILLUSIONS: A Psychological Study. By JAMES SULLY. $1.50.

XXXIV. THE SUN. By C. A. YOUNG, Professor of Astronomy in the College of New Jersey. With numerous Illustrations. $2.00.

New York: D. APPLETON & CO., 1, 3, & 5 Bond Street.

XXXV. VOLCANOES: What they Are and what they Teach. By JOHN W. JUDD, F. R. S., Professor of Geology in the Royal School of Mines. With 96 Illustrations. $2.00.

XXXVI. SUICIDE: An Essay in Comparative Moral Statistics. By HENRY MORSELLI, M. D., Professor of Psychological Medicine, Royal University, Turin. $1.75.

XXXVII. THE FORMATION OF VEGETABLE MOULD, THROUGH THE ACTION OF WORMS. With Observations on their Habits. By CHARLES DARWIN, LL. D., F. R. S., author of "On the Origin of Species," etc., etc. With Illustrations. $1.50.

XXXVIII. THE CONCEPTS AND THEORIES OF MODERN PHYSICS. By J. B. STALLO. $1.75.

XXXIX. THE BRAIN AND ITS FUNCTIONS. By J. LUYS. $1.50.

XL. MYTH AND SCIENCE. An Essay. By TITO VIGNOLI. $1.50.

THE INTERNATIONAL SCIENTIFIC SERIES.

DISEASES OF MEMORY:

AN ESSAY IN THE POSITIVE PSYCHOLOGY.

BY

TH. RIBOT,

AUTHOR OF

"HEREDITY: A PSYCHOLOGICAL STUDY OF ITS PHENOMENA, LAWS, CAUSES, AND CONSEQUENCES;" "ENGLISH PSYCHOLOGY;" ETC.

TRANSLATED FROM THE FRENCH,

BY WILLIAM HUNTINGTON SMITH.

NEW YORK:

D. APPLETON AND COMPANY,

1, 3, AND 5 BOND STREET.

1882.

PREFACE.

My purpose in this work is to provide a psychological monograph upon the diseases of memory, and, so far as the present state of our knowledge will permit, to derive from them certain deductions. The phenomena of memory have often been investigated, but never from a pathological stand-point. It has seemed to me that it might be profitable to consider the subject in this form. I have endeavored to limit myself to that, and have said nothing of the normal phases of memory, save so far as was necessary to make my meaning clear. I have cited many illustrations; this method, not in keeping with a purely literary study, is alone adapted to instruction. To write in a general way of the disorders of memory, without citing examples of each, would be, it seems to me, a useless task, since it is essential that the author's conclusions should be verified at every point. I beg the reader to note that he is offered here an essay in descriptive psychology, nothing more; and, if it has no other merit, this volume will bring to his attention many accounts of peculiar cases, scattered over a wide field of research, and only now brought together in a connected form.

T. R.

TABLE OF CONTENTS.

CHAPTER PAGE

I.—MEMORY AS A BIOLOGICAL FACT 9

Memory is essentially a biological fact, accidentally a psychical fact—Organic memory—Seat of memory—Modifications of nervous elements; dynamical associations between these elements—Conscious memory—Conditions of consciousness: intensity; duration—Unconscious cerebration—Nervous action is the fundamental condition of perception; consciousness is only an accessory—Localization in the past, or recollection—Mechanism of this operation—It is not a simple and instantaneous act; it consists of the addition of secondary states of consciousness to the principal state of consciousness—Memory is a vision in time—Localization, theoretical and practical—Reference points—Resemblance and difference between localization in the future and in the past—All memory an illusion—Forgetfulness a condition of memory—Return to the opening proposition: conscious memory tends little by little to become automatic.

II.—GENERAL AMNESIA 69

Classification of the diseases of memory—Temporary amnesia—Epileptics—Forgetfulness of certain periods of life—Examples of re-education—Slow and sudden recoveries—Case of provisional memory—Periodical or intermittent amnesia—Formation of two memories, totally or partially, distinct—Hypnotism—Progressive amnesia—Its importance: reveals the law which governs the destruction of memory—Law of regression; enunciation of this law—In

CHAPTER PAGE

what order memory fails—Counter-proof: it is re-formed in inverse order—Illustrations—Congenital amnesia—Extraordinary memory of idiots.

III.—PARTIAL AMNESIA 135

Reduction of memory to memories—Anatomical and physiological reasons for partial memories—Amnesia of numbers, names, figures, etc.—Amnesia of signs—Its nature: a loss of motor-memory—Examination of this point—Progressive amnesia of signs verifies completely the law of regression—Order of dissolution: proper names; common nouns; verbs and adjectives; interjections and language of sentiment; gestures—Relation between this dissolution and the evolution of the Indo-European languages—Counter-proof: return of signs in inverse order.

IV.—EXALTATIONS OF MEMORY 174

General excitation—Partial excitation—Return of lost impressions—Return of forgotten languages—Application to this fact of the law of regression—Case of perverted memory—Examples and explanations.

V.—CONCLUSION 192

Relations between the conservation of perceptions and nutrition, between the reproduction of impressions and the general and local circulation—Influence of the quantity and quality of the blood—Examples—The law of regression connected with a physiological principle and a psychological principle—Recapitulation.

DISEASES OF MEMORY.

CHAPTER I.

MEMORY AS A BIOLOGICAL FACT.

THE descriptive study of the phenomena of recollection has been often made by various authors, particularly by the Scotch; hence, this work will not attempt to cover that ground. I propose to ascertain what light the new method in psychology can throw upon the nature of memory; to show that the teachings of physiology, united with those of intuitive perception, lead us to state the problem in a much more comprehensive form; that memory, as ordinarily known to us and as psychology commonly describes it, far from comprising the whole process of memory, is only its most highly developed and complex phase, and that, taken by itself and studied alone, it is not easily understood; that it is the last term in a long evolutionary series, the product of an extended, but connected, development, having its origin in organic life; in short, that memory is, *per se*, a biological fact —by accident, a psychological fact.

Thus understood, our study comprises the physiology and psychology of memory, as well as its pathology. The disorders and maladies of this faculty, when classified and properly interpreted, are no longer to be regarded as a collection of amusing anecdotes of only passing interest. They will be found to be regulated by certain laws which constitute the very basis of memory, and from which its mechanism is easily laid bare.

I.

By common usage the word *memory* has a triple meaning: the conservation of certain conditions, their reproduction, and their localization in the past. This, however, is only a certain kind of memory, which we call perfect. The three elements are of unequal value: the first two are necessary, indispensable; the third, what in the language of the schools is called "recollection," completes the act of memory, but does not constitute it. Suppress the first two, and memory is annihilated; suppress the third, and memory ceases to exist in an objective, but not in a subjective, sense. This third element, which is purely psychological, would appear, then, to be superadded to the others: they are stable; it is unstable; it appears and disappears; it represents the extent of consciousness in the act of memory, and nothing more.

If memory is studied, as it has been up to this time, as "a faculty of the mind," by the aid of instinct alone, it is inevitable that this perfect and conscious form should be regarded as the whole of memory; but this is taking a part for the whole, or rather the species for the genus. Contemporary authors, such as Huxley, Clifford, and Maudsley, in maintaining that consciousness is only an adjunct of certain nervous processes, as incapable of reacting upon them as is a shadow upon the steps of the traveler whom it accompanies, have opened the way for a new theory which we shall attempt to formulate here. Let us set aside the psychical element for the time being, reduce the problem to its simplest terms, and try to discover how, without the aid of consciousness, a new condition is implanted in the organism, is conserved and reproduced; in other words, how memory is formed, independently of all cognition.

Before considering the real organic memory, it would be well to mention some of the views already advanced with regard to its constitution. Analogies to memory have been sought in the order of inorganic phenomena, particularly "in the property possessed by light of being stored up in a sheet of paper in a state of imperceptible vibration, for a greater or less time, ready to appear upon the application of a proper developing medium. Thus, engravings exposed to the solar rays and afterward kept in darkness will reveal, at the end of several months, by the aid of special reagents, permanent traces of the photographic action of the sun."* Lay a key upon a sheet of white paper exposed to the sunlight, place the paper in a dark drawer, and the spectral image of the key will still be visible after the lapse of years. † In our opinion, these and similar facts have too vague an analogy with memory to be of value as practical illustrations. Conservation, the first condition of recollection, is found, but that alone; for in these instances reproduction is so passive, so dependent upon the intervention of a foreign agent, that there is no resemblance to the natural reproduction of the memory. Hence, in studying our subject, it must never be forgotten that we have to do with vital laws, not with physical laws; and that the bases of memory must be looked for in the properties of organic matter, and nowhere else. We shall see, farther on, that those who forget this go wide of the mark. Neither shall I dwell upon phases of vegetable

* Luys, "Le Cerveau et ses Fonctions," p. 106.

† G. H. Lewes, "Problems of Life and Mind," third series, p. 57.

growth, which have been compared with the functions of memory, but hasten at once to decisive facts.

A general idea of the manner in which new functions are acquired, retained, and automatically reproduced, may be obtained from the muscular tissue of the animal kingdom. "Experience teaches us daily," says Hering, "that a muscle becomes stronger in proportion to its use. Muscular fiber, responding feebly at first to the excitation transmitted by the motor nerve, does so more vigorously the more frequently it is stimulated, allowing natural periods of repose. After each action it is better prepared for action, more disposed to a repetition of the same work, readier to reproduce a given organic process. It gains more in activity than in repose. We have here, in the simplest form, the nearest approach in physical conditions to that faculty of reproduction which is found in a state so complex in nerve-matter. What is observed in muscular tissue is found, to a greater or less extent, in the substance of other organs. Everywhere we perceive, with an increase of activity and proper intervals of repose, an increased power in organic functions."*

* Hering, "Ueber das Gedächtniss als allgemeine Function der organisirten Materie. Vortrag," etc., 2e Auflage, Wien, Gerold's Sohn, 1876, p. 13.

The most highly developed tissue of the organism, the nervous tissue, has, to an extreme degree, this double power of conservation and reproduction. We must not, however, look for the type of organic memory in the simple form of reflex action. Reflex action, whether it consists of an excitation followed by one or many contractions, is the result of structural tendency. It is reasonable to suppose that this anatomical predisposition is the product of heredity—that is to say, of a specific memory, acquired, fixed, and made organic by incessant repetition. But we shall not attempt to make this a valid argument in favor of our theory, since there are others less open to dispute.

The true type of organic memory—and here we enter the heart of our subject—must be sought in the group of facts to which Hartley has given the appropriate title of secondary automatic actions, as opposed to those automatic functions which are primitive or innate. These secondary automatic actions, or acquired movements, are the very basis of our every-day existence. Thus locomotion, which in many inferior species is innate, must be acquired by man, particularly the power of co-ordination which maintains the equilibrium of the body in any position, through the combination of tactile and visual impressions. In a general way, it may be said that the limbs and other sensorial organs of the adult act with facility only because of the sum of acquired and co-ordinate movements which forms for each part of the body its special memory, the accumulated capital upon which it lives, and through which it acts—just as the mind lives and acts in the medium of past experience. To the same category belong those groups of movements of a more artificial character which constitute the apprenticeship of the manual laborer, and are called into action in games of skill, bodily exercises, etc.

If we study the manner in which these primitive automatic movements are acquired, fixed, and reproduced, we see that the first requisite is the formation of associations. The original material is provided by primitive reflex actions, which must be properly grouped, some combined and others excluded. This formative period is one of constant experiment. Acts which seem now a part of our natures were originally acquired with difficulty. When light first strikes the eyes of a new-born child, an incoherent fluctuation of movements is observed; at the expiration of a few weeks the movements are co-ordinated, the eyes have the power of accommodation, and, being fixed upon a luminous point, are able to follow it with precision. When a child learns to write, according to Lewes, it is impossible for him to use his hand alone; he must also move his tongue, the facial muscles, and perhaps his feet.* In time he is able to suppress these useless discharges. And so, when we attempt for the first time any muscular act, we expend a great quantity of superfluous energy, which we learn gradually to subdue. By exercise, certain movements are fixed to the exclusion of others. Thus there are formed, in the nervous elements corresponding to the motor organs, secondary dynamical associations, more or less stable (that is to say, a memory), which unite with the primitive and permanent anatomical associations.

If the reader will observe these numerous and well-known secondary automatic actions, he will find that the organic memory thus formed resembles the psychological memory in all but one point—the absence of consciousness. Let us sum up their characteristics; the resemblance between the two will be readily apparent.

Acquisition, sometimes immediate, sometimes gradual; repetition of the act necessary in some cases, useless in others; an inequality of the organic memory according to individuals—it is rapid with some, slow, or totally refractory, with others (awkwardness is the result of a deficient organic memory). With some, associations once formed are permanent; with others, they are

* *Op. cit.*, p. 51.

easily lost or forgotten. We observe the arrangement of actions in simultaneous or successive series, as if for conscious recollection, and here is a fact worthy of careful notice: each member of the series *suggests* what is to follow; this is what happens when we walk without concerning ourselves with the movements of our limbs. Overcome with sleep, soldiers on foot as well as on horseback have continued to keep their places on the march, although those in the saddle were obliged to hold themselves in constant equilibrium. This power of organic suggestion is still more strikingly seen in a case cited by Carpenter,* of an accomplished pianist who rendered a piece of music while asleep, a fact which must be ascribed less to the sense of hearing than to the muscular sense which suggested the succession of movements. Without seeking extraordinary illustrations, we find in every-day life series of organic, complex, and carefully determined acts, with fixed limits, whose terms, all differing from one another, follow in constant order; for example, the ascent and descent of a staircase with which we are familiar. Our psychological memory is ignorant of the number of steps; but the organic memory knows this, as well as the number of flights, the arrangement of the landings, and other details;

* "Mental Physiology," p. 75, § 71.

it is never deceived. May we not say that to the organic memory these definite series are precisely analogous to a phrase, a couplet of verse, or a musical air to the psychological memory?

In its method of acquisition, conservation, and reproduction, we find, then, that the organic memory is identical with that of the mind. Consciousness alone is wanting. At the beginning it accompanies motor activity; then it is gradually effaced. Sometimes—and such cases are very instructive—its disappearance is sudden. A man subject to temporary suspensions of consciousness continued, during the stage of insensibility, any act already begun; on one occasion, while walking, he fell into the water. He was a shoemaker, and often wounded his fingers with his awl, continuing the action as if piercing leather.* In cases of the epileptic vertigo, known as "petit mal," similar facts are observed. A musician, who played the violin in an orchestra, was frequently seized with the momentary loss of consciousness, incident to this affection, during the performance of a selection. "He continued to play, however, and, although remaining in absolute ignorance of his surroundings, although he neither saw nor heard those whom he accompanied, he followed the measure."† In

* Carpenter, "Mental Physiology," p. 75.

† Trousseau, "Leçons cliniques," t. ii, xli, § 2. Many similar

such cases it seems as if consciousness had taken upon itself the task of exposing its own peculiar sphere, of reducing its *rôle* to proper proportions, and of showing, by sudden absence, the supplementary part which it plays in the mechanism of memory.

We are now prepared to advance further and ask what modifications of the organization are necessary for the establishment of a memory; what changes are undergone by the nervous system when a group of movements is definitively organized. We here reach the final question, warranted by facts, which can be propounded with regard to the organic bases of memory; and, if organic memory is a property of animal life, of which psychological memory is only a particular phase, all that we are able to discover or conjecture with regard to its ultimate conditions will apply equally well to memory as a whole.

It is impossible in such a research to avoid hypothesis. But, by evading all *à priori* conceptions, in holding rigidly to the facts, in resting upon what we know of nervous action, we avoid any likelihood of gross error. Our hypothesis, moreover, is capable of incessant modification. Finally, it will substitute in the mind,

facts of interest will be found in this work. We shall return to it in speaking of the pathology of memory.

for a vague phrase upon the conservation and reproduction of memory, a clear representation of the extremely complex process which produces and sustains it.

The first point to be established is with regard to the seat of memory. This question can give no room for serious controversy. The law, as formulated by Bain, is that "the renewed feeling occupies the very same parts, and in the same manner, as the original feeling." To give a striking example: experiment shows that the persistent idea of a brilliant color fatigues the optic nerve. We know that the perception of a colored object is often followed by a consecutive sensation which shows us the object with the same outline, but in a complementary color. It may be the same in the memory. It leaves, although with less intensity, a consecutive image. If with closed eyes we keep before the imagination a bright-colored figure for a long time, and then suddenly open the eyes upon a white surface, we may see for an instant the imaginary object with a complementary color. This fact, noted by Wundt, from whom we borrow it, proves that the nervous process is the same in both cases—in perception and in remembrance.*

We now begin to see more clearly into the

* For further details on this point, see Bain, "The Senses and the Intellect," p. 358.

problem of the physiological conditions of memory. These conditions are:

1. A particular modification impressed upon the nervous elements.

2. An association, a specific connection established between a given number of elements.

This second condition has not received the attention which it merits, as we shall endeavor to show.

To keep for the present to the organic memory, let us take one of the secondary automatic movements which have served as a type, and consider what takes place during the period of organization; let us take, for example, the movements of the lower limbs in locomotion.

Each movement requires the operation of a certain number of muscles, tendons, joints, ligaments, etc. These modifications—for the most part, at least—are transmitted to the sensorium. Whatever opinion may be held with regard to the anatomical conditions of muscular sensibility, it is certain that the sensibility exists, and that it makes known the part of the body participating in a movement, and permits us to regulate it.

What does this fact show? It implies modifications received and conserved by a determined group of nervous elements. "The movements that are instigated or actuated by a particular nervous center do, like the idea, leave behind them residua, which, after several repetitions, become so completely organized into the nature of the nervous center that the movements may henceforth be automatic." * "The residua of volitions, like the residua of sensations or ideas, remain in the mind and render future volitions of a like kind more easy and more definite."† By this organization of residua, after the period of experiment of which we have spoken, we are able to execute movements with facility and increasing precision, until they finally become automatic.

Submitting this familiar instance of organic memory to analysis, we see that it implies the two conditions mentioned above.

The first is a particular modification impressed upon the nervous elements. As this has been often discussed, it need not detain us. But does the nervous fiber, in receiving an entirely new impression, retain a permanent modification? This point is disputed. Some regard the nerves as simple conductors, whose constituent matter, disturbed for a moment, returns to a state of primitive equilibrium. Whether transmission is explained by longitudinal vibration in the axis-cylinder, or the chemical decomposition of pro-

* Maudsley, "Physiology and Pathology of the Mind," p. 167.
† Idem, p. 157.

toplasm, it is difficult to believe that no trace remains. We find at least in the nerve-cell an element which, by common consent, receives, stores up, and reacts. Now, an impression once received leaves its imprints. Hence, according to Maudsley, there is produced an aptitude, and with that a differentiation of the element, although we have no reason to think that originally it differed from homologous cells. "Every impression leaves a certain ineffaceable trace; that is to say, molecules once disarranged and forced to vibrate in a different way can not return exactly to their primitive state. If I brush the surface of water at rest with a feather, the liquid will not take again the form which it had before; it may again present a smooth surface, but molecules will have changed places, and an eye of sufficient power would see traces of the passage of the feather. Organic molecules acquire a greater or less degree of aptitude for submitting to disarrangement. No doubt, if this same exterior force did not again act upon the same molecules, they would tend to return to their natural form; but it is far otherwise if the action is several times repeated. In this case they lose, little by little, the power of returning to their original form, and become more and more closely identified with that which is forced upon them, until this becomes natural in its turn, and they again obey the least cause that will set them in vibration." *

It is impossible to say in what this modification consists. Neither the microscope, nor reagents, nor histology, nor histochemistry can reveal it; but facts and reason indicate that it takes place.

The second condition, which consists in the establishment of stable associations between different groups of nervous elements, has up to this time received but little attention. I do not find that contemporary authors even have realized its importance. It is, however, a necessary corollary to their thesis upon the seat of memory.

Some seem to admit, at least by implications, that an organic or conscious remembrance is impressed upon a given cell, which, with its nervous filaments, has in a certain sense a monopoly of conservation and reproduction. I believe that this illusion has in part arisen through indefinite language, which leads us to regard a movement, a perception, an idea, an image, a sentiment, as *one* thing, as a *unity*. Reflection will show, however, that each of these supposed unities is composed of numerous and heterogeneous elements; that it is an association, a group, a fusion, a complexus, a

* Delbœuf, "Théorie générale de la sensibilité," p. 60.

multiplicity. To return to the example cited above—that of locomotion: each movement may be considered as reflex action of a very complicated order, of which the contact of the foot with the ground is at every moment the initial impression.

Let us take this movement in its complete form. Is the starting-point an act of volition? Then the impulse, originating, according to Ferrier, in a particular portion of the cortex, traverses the white substance, reaches the corpora striata, passes through the crura cerebri, thence to the complicated structure of the medulla, where it passes to the other side of the body, descending the anterior columns of the spinal cord to the lumbar region, and then along the motor nerves to the muscles. This transmission is followed by a return to the cerebral center, through the posterior columns of the cord and the gray matter, the medulla, the pons varolii, the optic tract and the white substance, to the surface of the hemisphere. Take this movement in its abridged and ordinary form when its character is entirely automatic. Then the course is simply from the periphery to the cerebral ganglia, to return again to the periphery, the upper portion of the brain remaining inactive.

This course—whose principal points have

been roughly indicated, and all of whose details are not known, even by the most learned anatomists—presupposes the activity of a very large number of nervous elements, all differing from one another. Thus the motor and sympathetic nerves differ in structure from those of the brain and spinal cord. The cells differ from one another in volume, in form, in arrangement, in the number of filaments, and in their position in the cerebro-spinal axis, since they extend from the lower extremity of the spinal cord to the cerebral layers. Each of these elements has a part to play. If the reader will cast his eyes over an anatomical chart or a few histological plates, he will obtain an approximate idea of the immense number of nervous elements necessary for the production of a movement, and therefore for its conservation and reproduction.

It is of the highest importance that attention should be given to this point, viz.: that organic memory supposes not only a modification of nervous elements, *but the formation among them of determinate associations for each particular act*, the establishment of certain *dynamic* affinities, which, by repetition, become as stable as the primitive anatomical connections. In our opinion, the important feature with regard to the basis of memory is not only the modification impressed upon each element, but the manner in which a number of elements group themselves together and form a complexus.

This point being to us of capital importance, we may be permitted to enlarge upon it. We may note first that our hypothesis—a necessary consequence of admitted facts concerning the seat of memory—really obviates certain difficulties while apparently introducing new complications. The question arises whether each nerve-cell is able to retain several different modifications; or if, once modified, it is permanently polarized. Naturally, we fall back on conjecture. We must believe that, if each cell is capable of modifications, the number is limited. We may even admit that there is only one. The number of cerebral cells being, according to Meynert's calculations, 600,000,000 (and Sir Lionel Beale gives a much larger estimate), the hypothesis of a single impression is not untenable. But this question has for us a secondary interest; for, even admitting the last hypothesis —the most unfavorable for the explanation of the number and complexity of organized memories — we see that this single modification may enter into different combinations, and produce different results. We must not only take into account each individual factor, but its relations and the resulting combinations. We may compare the modified cell to a letter of the alphabet; this letter, always preserving its own identity, aids in the formation of millions of words in many languages, living and dead. By proper association, numerous and complex combinations may be derived from a small number of elements. To return to our example of locomotion: organic memory, which forms its basis, consists of a particular modification of a great many nervous elements. But many of these elements, so modified, may serve another purpose, enter into new combinations, and form another memory. The secondary automatic movements employed in swimming or dancing require certain modifications of the muscles and articulations already used in locomotion, already registered in certain nervous elements: they find, in fact, a memory already organized, many of whose elements are turned to their own use, causing them to enter into new combinations and concur in the formation of another memory.

Note, again, that the necessity for a great number of cells and nerve-filaments for the conservation and reproduction of a movement, however simple, implies an equally great possibility of permanence and revivification; in consequence of the number of elements, and the stability of their association, the chances of reanimation are increased, each being able to contribute something to the revival of the others.

Finally, our hypothesis is in accord with two facts of common observation.

1. An acquired movement, well fixed in the organism, well *learned*, is with difficulty replaced by another having nearly the same form, but requiring a different mechanism. It is a question of destroying one association and building up another; of breaking relations already established and forming new ones.

2. It sometimes happens that in place of one accustomed movement we involuntarily produce another, which is explained by the fact that the same elements, entering into the different combinations, are able to sustain discharges in different directions, and that an infinitely small circumstance suffices to set one group in action in place of another, and thus produce different results.

On this theory we explain the following incident recorded by Lewes:* "I was one day relating a visit to the Epileptic Hospital, and, intending to name the friend, Dr. Bastian, who accompanied me, I said, 'Dr. Brinton,' then immediately corrected this with 'Dr. Bridges'; this also was rejected, and 'Dr. Bastian' was pronounced. I was under no confusion whatever

* *Op. cit.*, p. 128.

as to the persons, but, having imperfectly adjusted the group of muscles necessary for the articulation of the one name, the one element which was common to that group and to the others, namely, B, served to recall all three." This explanation seems perfectly exact, and we again note with this author a well-known fact which will support our theory. "Who does not know how, in trying to recollect a name, we are tormented with the sense of its beginning with a certain letter, and how, by keeping this letter constantly before the mind, at last the whole group emerges?"* An analogous remark might be made concerning the acquired movements employed in writing. It is a mistake which I have often observed myself when writing rapidly or with a fatigued brain; it is so brief, so quickly repaired, and so soon forgotten, that the examples given were noted at once. Wishing to write "*doit de bonnes*," I wrote "*donne.*" Wishing to write "*ne* pas *faire une part*," I wrote "*ne* part *faire*," etc., etc. Evidently in the first instance the letter D, and in the second the letter P (I express by these symbols the psycho-physiological state which served as the basis of their conception and graphic reproduction)—in each instance the letter in question excited one group instead of another; and this confusion

* *Op. cit.*, pp. 128, 129.

was the easier since the remainder of the groups, "*onne*," "*art*," were already consciously evolved. I believe that those who will take the trouble to observe carefully their own errors of this sort will not deny that the fact is of frequent occurrence.

It must not be forgotten that the preceding is an hypothesis; but it apparently conforms to scientific data, and accounts for the facts. It permits the representation, in intelligible form, of the bases of organic memory, the acquired movements which constitute the memory of different organs—the eyes, hands, arms, and legs. These bases do not, in our opinion, consist of a purely mechanical registration, or, according to a popular view, of an imprint, preserved we know not where, like that of the key on the sheet of paper. These are metaphors which have no place here. Memory is a biological fact. A rich and extensive memory is not a collection of impressions, but an accumulation of dynamical associations, very stable and very responsive to proper stimuli.

II.

We have now to consider a more complex form of memory—that which is accompanied by acts of consciousness, and which even many psychologists are apt to regard as constituting its entire function. Let us see how far what has been said of organic memory is applicable here, and the added effect of consciousness itself. In passing from the simple to the complex, from the lower to the higher, from the stable to the unstable form of memory, it is impossible to avoid the question as to the relation between unconsciousness and consciousness. The problem is so involved in natural obscurity and artificial mysticism that it is almost impossible to deal with it in clear and positive terms. We will make the attempt, however.

It is very evident at the beginning that we have no concern with the metaphysics of unconsciousness as conceived by Hartmann and others. We may even declare at once that we see no way of explaining the transition from unconsciousness to consciousness. We may indulge in plausible and ingenious hypotheses, but nothing more. However, psychology as a practical science has nothing to fear. It takes certain states of consciousness for granted, without occupying itself with their genesis. All that it can do is to determine some of the conditions in which they exist.

The first of these conditions is the mode of activity of the nervous system termed by physiologists the nervous discharge. But the greater portion of nervous states either do not assist in the evolution of consciousness, or contribute to it in a very indirect way; for instance, the excitations and discharges in the great sympathetic; the normal action of the vaso-motor nerves; many of the reflex nerves, etc. Others are accompanied by consciousness at intermittent stages; or, being conscious in early life, cease to be so in the adult state; the secondary automatic actions, of which we have spoken, are examples. Nervous activity is much more extended than psychical activity; every psychical action presupposes a nervous action, but the reverse is by no means true. Between that form of nervous activity which is never, or hardly ever, accompanied by consciousness, and the form of nervous activity which is always, or nearly always, so accompanied—between these two classes lies a third, where consciousness is sometimes present and sometimes absent. In this group unconsciousness is to be studied.

Before proceeding farther with this subject, let us consider again two conditions of the existence of consciousness—intensity, and duration.

1. Intensity is a condition of extremely variable character. States of consciousness are continually striving to supplant it, but the victory may result either from the strength of the victor or the weakness of the other combatants. We know—and this point has been made very

clear by Herbart and others — that the most exalted state may continue to decrease until the threshold of consciousness is passed—that is to say, until one of the conditions of existence fails. We are justified in saying that there may be every possible degree of consciousness, as small as desired, to the lowest modality—conditions named by Maudsley subconscious—but there is no authority for believing that this decrease has no limit, even although it escapes us.

2. Little attention has been paid to *duration* as a necessary condition of consciousness. It is, however, of capital importance. Here we are able to reason from exact data. Thirty years of investigation have determined the time required for different perceptions (sound, 0″·16 to 0″·14; touch, 0″·21 to 0″·18; light, 0″·20 to 0″·22; for the simplest act of discernment, the nearest to reflex action, 0″·02 to 0″·04). Although the results vary with the person, the circumstances, and the nature of the psychical acts under investigation, it is at least proved that every psychical act requires an appreciable duration of time, and that "the infinite speed of thought" is only a metaphor. This known, it is evident that every nervous action whose duration is less than that required for psychical action can not arouse consciousness. In this

connection it is instructive to examine the nervous action accompanying a state of purely reflex consciousness. According to Exner,* the physiological time necessary for a reflex action must be from 0″·0662 to 0″·0578—a number much less than those given above for different orders of perception. If, as Herbert Spencer says, the wing of a fly makes from ten to fifteen thousand vibrations per second,† and each vibration implies a separate nervous action, we have an example of a nervous state whose rapidity is astounding, compared with which a nervous state accompanied by consciousness occupies an enormous period of time. As a result of the foregoing, it is evident that every state of consciousness necessarily occupies a certain duration, and that an essential condition of consciousness is wanting when the duration of the nervous process falls below this minimum.‡

* Pflüger's "Archiv.," viii (1874), p. 526. The duration of reflex action varies with the exciting force, and according to whether transmission in the spinal cord is longitudinal or transverse. This subject is far from being exhausted.

† According to Marey, the wing of a fly vibrates only 330 times per second. This discrepancy, however, does not affect the validity of our reasoning.

‡ The determination of the duration of psychical acts will throw much light upon facts connected with mental activity. In my opinion, it will also contribute to the explanation of the changes from consciousness to unconsciousness in acquired movements. An act is first executed slowly and consciously; by repetition we gain ease and rapidity; that is, the nervous process

The question of unconsciousness is only vague and embarrassed by contradictory opinions because badly stated. If we consider consciousness as an essence, a fundamental property of the mind, all is obscure; if we consider it as a phenomenon having its own conditions of existence, all becomes clear, and unconsciousness is no longer a mystery. It must not be forgotten that a state of consciousness is a complex modality requiring a particular condition of the nervous system; that this nervous action is not accessory, but an integral part of the given state—its basis, the fundamental condition of its existence; that, from the moment it is produced, this state exists in and of itself; that when consciousness is added the state still exists in and of itself; that consciousness completes, finishes, but does not constitute it. If one of the conditions of consciousness is wanting, whether intensity, or duration, or others of which we are ignorant, a part of this complex phenomenon — consciousness — disappears; but another part—the nervous process—remains. There is left of the action only its organic phase. It is not surprising, then, that, later on, results of cerebral activity should become manifest;

which serves as a base, finding a path already marked out, moves more rapidly, until it gradually falls below the minimum necessary for consciousness.

they already existed, but in an undeveloped form.

This understood, everything that pertains to unconscious activity loses its mysterious character and is explained with the greatest ease: for instance, the spontaneous acts of memory, which appear to be incited by no association, and which are experienced daily by every one; a student's lessons, read at night and found to be fully mastered the following day; problems long pondered over, whose solution suddenly flashes on the consciousness; poetic, scientific, and mechanical inventions; strange feelings of sympathy or antipathy, etc. Unconscious cerebration does its work noiselessly, and sets obscure ideas in order. In a curious case related by Dr. Holmes* and cited by Carpenter, a man had a vague knowledge of the work going on in his brain, without attaining to the state of distinct consciousness: "A business man in Boston, . . . having an important question under consideration, had given it up for the time as too much for him. But he was conscious of an action going on in his brain which was so unusual and painful as to excite his apprehensions that he was threatened with palsy, or something of that sort. After some hours of this uneasiness, his perplexity was all at once cleared up by the natural solution of his

* "Mechanism in Thought and Morals," p. 47.

doubts coming to him—worked out, as he believed, in that obscure and troubled interval." *

In summing up, we may picture the nervous system as traversed by continuous discharges. Among these nervous actions some respond to the endless rhythm of the vital functions; others, fewer in number, to the succession of states of consciousness; still others, by far the most numerous, to unconscious cerebration. Six hundred millions (or twelve hundred millions) of cells, and four or five thousands of millions of fibers, even deducting those in repose or which remain inactive during a lifetime, offer a sufficient contingent of active elements. The brain is like a laboratory full of movement, where thousands of occupations are going on at once. Unconscious cerebration, not being subject to restrictions of time, operating, so to speak, only in space, may act in several directions at the same moment.

* Carpenter, "Mental Physiology," p. 533. The whole chapter contains interesting facts with regard to unconscious cerebration. A mathematician, a friend of the author, was occupied with a geometrical problem whose solution he failed of obtaining after a number of trials. Several years later the correct solution flashed upon his mind so suddenly that he "trembled as if in the presence of another being who had communicated the secret" (p. 536). If any one wishes to behold the spectacle of a powerful and penetrating mind hampered by a bad method, let him read Sir William Hamilton's remarkable study on "Latency" ("Lectures on Metaphysics," v. i, Lect. xviii). With his theory of the psychical faculties, and his willful neglect of physiology, he was unable to cope with such questions.

Consciousness is the narrow gate through which a very small part of all this work is able to reach us.

We have just determined the relation of consciousness to unconsciousness; in the same manner we may know the relation of psychical memory to organic memory: one is only a special phase of the other. What has been said of physiological memory applies in a general way to conscious memory; only a single factor is added. It is worth while, however, to take up the question anew and consider it in detail. The subject has again a twofold aspect: we are to examine into the residua, and the manner in which they are associated.

I. The old theories upon memory, having regard only to its psychological meaning, assigned as its base "vestiges," "traces," or "residua," and often used these terms in an equivocal sense. Sometimes it was a question of material imprints on the brain, sometimes of latent modifications stored up in the "mind." Those who adopted the last view were logical. But this theory, although it has many supporters among those who ignore physiology, is untenable. A state of consciousness which is not consciousness, a representation which is not represented, is a pure *flatus vocis*. Take away from anything that which constitutes its reality, and you reduce it to a possibility; that is to say, when the conditions of existence reappear, it will reappear; which brings us back to the theory advanced above with regard to unconsciousness.

With us the problem of "psychological residua" is solved in advance; if every state of consciousness implies as an integral part a nervous action, and, if this action produces a permanent modification of the nervous centers, the state of consciousness will also be recorded in the same place and manner. The objection may be raised, indeed, that a state of consciousness implies a nervous action *and something more.* But that does not affect our position. If the primitive nervous state—that which responds to perception—is sufficient to sustain this "something more," the secondary nervous state—that which responds to remembrance—is also sufficient. The conditions are the same in each instance, and the solution of the difficulty, if a solution is possible, must be sought in a theory of perception, not in a theory of memory.

This psycho-physiological residue we may style with Wundt a *disposition*, and note with him in what it differs from an imprint. "Analogies borrowed from the domain of physiology emphasize this difference. When the eye is exposed to intense light, the sense-impression persists in the form of a consecutive image. The eye, each day comparing and measuring distances and relations in space, gains more and more in precision. The consecutive image is an imprint; the accommodation of the eye, its faculty of measurement, is a functional disposition. It may be that, in the case of the unexercised eye, the retina and the muscles are constituted the same as in the exercised organ, but there is in the second a disposition much more marked than in the first. No doubt the physiological tendency of any organ depends less upon its modifications, properly so called, than upon the imprints which remain in its nervous centers. But all physiological study relative to the phenomena of habit, adaptation to given conditions, etc., shows that these same imprints consist essentially in functional dispositions." *

II. These considerations bring us to the point upon which we wish to lay particular stress. Dynamical associations have a much more important part to play in conscious memory than in organic memory. We might repeat here what has been said before; but the question has been studied so little from this stand-point that it will be better to consider it in another form.

Each of us has in his consciousness a certain number of recollections: images of men, animals, cities, countries, facts of history, or sci-

* "Grundzüge der philosophischen Psychologie," p. 791.

ence or language. These recollections come back to us in the form of a more or less extended series. The formation of these series has been very clearly explained by the laws of association between different states of consciousness. We are now concerned, not with the series, but with their component terms. Let us analyze a state of simple consciousness and discern its complex meaning.

Take as one of these terms the memory of an apple. According to the verdict of consciousness, this is a simple fact. Physiology shows that this verdict is an illusion. The memory of an apple is necessarily a weakened form of the perception of an apple. What does this perception suppose? A modification of the complex structure of the retina, transmission by the optic nerve through the corpora geniculata and the tubercula quadrigemina to the cerebral ganglia (optic tract?), then through the white substance to the cortex. This supposes the activity of many widely separated elements. But this is by no means all. It is not a question of a simple sensation of color. We see, or imagine, the apple as a solid object having a spherical form. These conceptions result from the exquisite muscular sensibility of our visual apparatus and from its movements. Now, the movements of the eye are regulated by several nerves—the sympathetic, the oculo-motor, and its branches. Each of these nerves has its own termination, and is connected by a devious course with the outer cerebral layer, where the motor intuitions, according to Maudsley, are formed. We simply indicate outlines. For further details the reader should consult standard works on anatomy and physiology. But we have given an idea of the prodigious number of nervous filaments and distinct communities of cells scattered through the different parts of the cerebro-spinal axis, which serve as a basis for the psychical state known as the memory of an apple, and which the double illusion of consciousness and language leads us to consider as a simple fact.

Is it said that visual perception is too complex, and proves too much in favor of our theory? Then take the recollection of a word. If it is a written word it is again a question of visual perception, and is allied to the instance already cited. But if we take a spoken word we find the complexity equally great. Articulate language supposes the intervention of the larynx, the pharynx, the lips, the nasal fossa, and, consequently, of many nerves having centers in different parts of the brain—the spinal, the facial, and the hypoglossal. If we include auditory impressions in the memory of words, the complication is greater still. Then the cerebral center must be united with Broca's convolution and the island of Reil, universally considered as the psychical center of speech. We thus see that the case does not differ from the preceding, either in nature or complexity, and that the memory of every word must have as its basis a determinate association of nervous elements.*

It is unnecessary to dwell upon this point. What has been said shows the importance of the associations which I call the dynamic bases of memory, the modifications impressed upon the elements being the static bases. Examples of more simple cases might be given, but they would be superfluous. The memory conserves and reproduces real, concrete states of consciousness; we must therefore consider them as such, and choose our illustrations from that order of phenomena. Psychological analysis and *idealogical* analysis may, each in its own province, descend to ultimate elements; it is a useful work to investigate the genesis of states of consciousness: here we consider them as already formed. When we begin to talk we use simple words; later, isolated phrases. For a long time we do

* Forbes Winslow ("On the Obscure Diseases of the Brain and Disorders of the Mind," 4th edition, p. 257) cites the case of a soldier who was trepanned, losing in the operation some portion of the brain. He forgot the numbers *five* and *seven*, and was not able to recollect them for a considerable time.

not realize that these words are made up of simple elements; many are always ignorant of the fact. Consciousness, which is an interior voice, is regulated by the same laws. The apparently simple is, on analysis, found to be complex. There can be no doubt that these simple states, which are the alphabet of consciousness, require for their conservation and reproduction certain nervous collocations. The facts already cited relative to letters and syllables offer sufficient proof. There is another more curious. "A man of scholastic attainments," says Forbes Winslow, "lost, after an attack of acute fever, all knowledge of the letter F." *

If, then, we would comprehend a "good memory," and translate this expression into physiological terms, we must imagine a great number of nervous elements, each modified in a special manner, each forming part of a distinct association and probably ready to enter into others; and each of these associations containing within itself the conditions essential to the existence of states of consciousness. Memory has, then, static and dynamic bases. Its power is in ratio with their number and stability.

* *Op. cit.*, p. 258. The author does not tell us whether it was the articulate sound or the written sign; or whether the patient recovered.

III.

We have now to study the real character of psychical memory to determine what alone belongs to a mental phase which, retaining all its essential parts and organic conditions, constitutes the most complex, the highest, and the most unstable form of memory. This, in the language of the schools, is called recollection. I shall call it localization in time, since the term implies no theory and is only a simple expression of facts. There are few questions which the scholastic method has embarrassed with more difficulties and factitious explanations. It will therefore be well to state in a few words how we regard the problem and its solution.

Localization in time (for instance, the recollection of something that happened, at what time and in what place) is not a primitive act. It supposes, aside from the principal state of consciousness, secondary states, variable in number and degree, which, by their groupings, operate as determinate causes. In our opinion the mechanism of recollection is best explained by the mechanism of vision.

The distinction between primitive and acquired sight-perceptions has been recognized since the time of Berkeley. We know that the primitive impression is that of color; that the secondary impressions are those of direction, extent, and form; that the first depends upon the sensibility of the retina, while the latter depend upon the muscular sensibility of the eye; and, finally, that through habit the primitive and the acquired are so confounded as to form in a general sense but one act, simple and immediate—although analysis, experiment, and pathological observation prove the contrary. It is the same with memory. First we have the primitive state of consciousness as a simple existence; secondary states of consciousness which follow and which provide the ideas of relation and judgment, localize it at a certain distance in the past; so that we may define memory as *a vision in time.* The phenomena thus outlined must now be considered more in detail.

The theoretical explanation of localization in time starts with the law, enunciated by Dugald Stewart and admirably explained by Taine, that imaginary acts are always accompanied by the belief (at least for the moment) in the existence of the corresponding reality.* This illusion, which exists in the highest degree in hallucination, vertigo, and dreams (for want of real perceptions to correct it) also exists, although in a less degree, in all states of consciousness. I

* Taine, "De l'Intelligence," 1re partie, livre ii, ch. i, § 3.—A collection of facts which leave no doubt upon the subject.

shall not now speak of the mechanism through which a conscious state is deprived of its objective reality and reduced to a purely mental perception, but refer the reader to the explanations given by M. Taine.*

These instances, however, are not recollections. So long as an image, whatever its content (whether it represent a house, or a mechanical invention, or a sentiment), remains isolated as if suspended in consciousness, with no relation to other states having a fixed position, incapable of classification—so long we regard it as a present existence. But among these mental images some have the power, from the moment they enter into consciousness, of pushing out ramifications in different directions and sustaining states which connect them with the present, and by which they appear to us as parts of a more or less extended series; in other words, they are localized in time.

I shall not attempt to determine whether memory is a postulate of the idea of time, or whether the idea of time is a postulate of memory; or whether time is a form *à priori* of mind; or whether it is explicable by experimental reasoning. These questions belong to the criticism of consciousness, and not to empirical psychology. The latter is not concerned with

* *Op. cit.*—particularly the second part, livre i, ch. ii.

critical or ontological discussions. It states as a simple fact that time implies memory, and that memory implies time. This is sufficient, and, being admitted, the question arises, How do we localize a given event in time?

Theoretically, in only one way. We determine position in time as we determine position in space—by reference to a fixed point, which, in the case of time, is the present. It must be observed that the present is a real existence, which has a given duration. However brief it may be, it is not, as the language of metaphor would lead us to believe, a flash, a nothing, an abstraction analogous to a mathematical point. It has a beginning and an end. But its beginning does not appear to us as an absolute beginning. It touches upon something with which it forms continuity. When we read or hear a sentence, for example, at the commencement of the fifth word something of the fourth still remains. Each state of consciousness is only progressively effaced; it leaves an evanescent trace, similar to that which, in the physiology of sight, is called an after-sensation. Hence, the fourth and fifth words are in continuity; the end of the one impinges upon the beginning of the other. That is the important fact. There is not an indeterminate contiguity of two *somethings;* but the *initial* point of one actual state touches the *final* point of the anterior state. If this simple fact is thoroughly understood, the theoretical mechanism of localization in time will be equally clear, for it is evident that the retrogressive transition may exist as well between the fourth word and the third, and that, each state of consciousness having its individual duration, the number of states so traversed, and the sum of their duration, will give the position of any state whatever with reference to the present, or its distance in time. Such is the theoretical mechanism of localization, namely, a retrogressive movement, which, starting from the present, traverses a more or less extended series of terms.

Practically, we have recourse to processes much more simple and expeditious. Rarely do we make this retrograde passage through all the intermediate terms, or even the greater part of them. Our way is facilitated by the use of reference points. I will cite a familiar instance. On the 30th of November I am looking for a book of which I have great need. It is coming from a distance, and its transportation will require at least twenty days. Did I send for it in time? After a little hesitation I remember that my order was given on the eve of a short journey, whose date I can fix in a precise manner as Sunday, the 9th of November. With this, recollection is complete. In analyzing this case, we observe that the principal state of consciousness—the order for the book—is first thrown into the past in an indeterminate manner. It arouses secondary states, compares them, and places itself before or after. "The image travels back and forth along the line of the past; every phrase mentally pronounced gives it a new impetus." * After a number of oscillations, more or less extended, it finds its place; it is fixed, remembered. In this example the recollection of the journey is what I designate as a reference point.

I understand by reference point an event, a state of consciousness, whose position in time we know—that is to say, its distance from the present moment, and by which we can measure other distances. These reference points are states of consciousness which, through their intensity, are able to survive oblivion, or, through their complexity, are of a nature to sustain many relations and to augment the chances of revivification. They are not arbitrarily chosen; they obtrude upon us. Their value is entirely relative. They are for an hour, a day, a week, a month; then, no longer used, they are forgotten. They have, as a general thing, a distinct individuality; some of them, however, are common

* Taine, *op. cit.*, second part, liv. i, ch. ii, § 7. An excellent analysis of a similar example will be found in this place.

to a family, a society, or a nation. These reference points form for each of us different series corresponding to the events that make up our life: daily occupations, domestic incidents, professional work, scientific investigations, etc., the series becoming more numerous as the life of the individual is more varied. These reference points are like mile-stones or guide-posts placed along the route, which, starting from a central place, diverge in different directions. There is always this peculiarity: that the series may, so to speak, be placed in juxtaposition and compared one with another.

It remains for us to show how these reference points permit us to simplify the mechanism of localization. The impression which we call a reference point returning, by hypothesis, very often to consciousness, is very often compared with the present according to its position in time—that is to say, intermediate states which separate them are more or less completely revived. As a result, the position of a reference point is, or seems to be (for we shall see further on that all recollection implies an illusion), better and better known. By repetition this localization becomes immediate, instantaneous, automatic. The process is analogous to the formation of acquired states (habits). The intermediate terms disappear because they are useless. The series is reduced to two terms, and these two terms suffice, since their distance in time is known. Without this abridged process and the disappearance of a prodigious number of terms, localization in time would be very long and tedious, and restricted to very narrow limits. By its aid, as soon as the image is formed, its primary localization is instantaneous; it is placed between two landmarks—the present and some given point of reference. The process is concluded after a few trials, often laborious, sometimes fruitless, and perhaps never precise.

If the reader will study carefully his own recollections, I do not believe that he will raise any serious objections to what has just been said. He will, moreover, note how this mechanism resembles that of localization in space. Here, also, we have our reference points, abridged methods, and well-known distances which we employ as units of measurement.

It will not be unprofitable to show in a few words that localization in the future is executed in an analogous manner. Our knowledge of the future can only be a copy of the past. I find only two categories of facts: those which are a reproduction, pure and simple, of what has occurred at similar epochs, in the same places under like circumstances; and those which consist of inductions, deductions, or conclusions, drawn from the past, but produced by the logical working of the mind. Outside of these two categories everything is possible, but everything is unknown.

Evidently the first class most nearly resembles memory, since it is a simple reproduction of what has been. A man is in the habit of going every year to pass the month of September at a country house. In the middle of winter he sees it with all its surroundings, inhabitants, and characteristic activity. This image is at first indeterminate; it is equally an object of remembrance and of the future. Then it glides away from the present through winter, spring, and summer; finally it is localized. The course of the year, with its succession of seasons, *fêtes*, and changes of occupation, provides reference points. The mechanism differs from that of memory only in one respect: we pass from the termination of the present to the beginning of the following state. We do not proceed, as in recollection, from beginning to end, but from end to beginning. Theoretically, we traverse in this invariable order all intermediate states; in fact, only the reference points. The mechanism is the same as that employed in memory, only it acts in a different direction.

To recapitulate: setting aside verbal explanations, we find that recollection is not a "faculty," but a fact, and that this fact is a result of aggregate conditions. As with recollection, localization in time varies through every possible degree according to the conditions. At the highest stage of development are the reference points; below those, rapid and precise recollections, located almost as quickly; one degree lower, those which cause hesitation, requiring an appreciable time; lower yet, laborious recollections, only attained by trial and stratagem; finally, in some instances, the labor is useless, and our indecision is translated into such phrases as, "It seems to me that I have seen that form!" "Did I dream that?" One step more, and localization is entirely wanting; the image, denied an abiding place, wanders in devious mazes, incapable of rest. There are many examples of this last case, and they are found in the least expected forms. Through the effects of disease or old age, celebrated men have been unable to recognize cherished works of their own production. Toward the close of his life Linnæus took great pleasure in perusing his own books, and when reading would cry out, forgetting that he was the author, "How beautiful! What would I not give to have written that!" A similar anecdote is told of Newton and the discovery of the differential calculus. Walter Scott as he grew old was subject to similar forgetfulness. One day some one recited in his presence a poem which pleased him much; he asked the author's name; it was a canto from his "Pirate." Ballantyne, who acted as his secretary and wrote his life, has related in the most circumstantial manner how the greater part of "Ivanhoe" was dictated during a severe illness. The book was finished and printed before the author was able to leave his bed. He retained no remembrance of it, except the main conception of the romance, which had been thought of prior to the attack.

In a case cited by Forbes Winslow, the image is apparently waiting to be seized and localized; it is on the edge of recognition; the smallest aid would suffice, but is wanting. A lady was driving out with the poet Rogers, then ninety years old, and asked him after an acquaintance whom he could not recollect. "He pulled the checkstring, and appealed to his servant. 'Do I know Lady M.?' The reply was, 'Yes, sir.' This was a painful moment to us both. Taking my hand, he said, 'Never mind, my dear, I am not yet compelled to stop the carriage and ask if I know you.'"*

A much more instructive instance is recorded

* Laycock, "Organic Laws of Personal and Ancestral Memory," p. 19; Carpenter, *op. cit.*, p. 444; Ballantyne, "Life of Walter Scott," ch. xliv; Spring, "Symptomology," vol. ii; Forbes Winslow, *op. cit.*, p. 247.

by Macaulay in his essay on Wycherley, whose memory, he tells us, was "at once preternaturally strong and preternaturally weak" in his declining years. If anything was read to him at night, he awoke the next morning with a mind overflowing with the thoughts and expressions heard the night before; and he wrote them down with the best faith in the world, nothing doubting that they were his own. Here the mechanism of memory was plainly dissevered; pathology provides us with an explanation. Interpreting the case according to principles already laid down, we should say: The modification impressed upon the cerebral cells was persistent; the dynamical associations of the nervous elements were stable; the state of consciousness connected with each was evolved; these states of consciousness were reassociated and constituted a series (phrases or verses). Then the mental operation was suddenly arrested. The series aroused no secondary state; they remained isolated with nothing to connect them with the present, with nothing by which they might be located in time. They remained in the condition of illusions; they seemed to be new because no concomitant state impressed upon them the imprint of the past.

Localization in time is so far from being a simple, primitive, instantaneous act, that it often requires an appreciable interval, even for consciousness. In cases where it is apparently instantaneous its rapidity is a result of repetition. The eye judges in the same way of the distances of objects, and it is probable that, in the case of a nascent memory as in that of nascent vision, localization is never instantaneous.* We have found, in fact, in the highest form of memory only one new operation—localization in time. In conclusion it remains for us to show the relatively illusory character of this process.

I recall at this moment very vividly a visit which I made a year ago to an old château in Bohemia. The visit lasted two hours. To-day I go over it again readily in imagination. I enter by the great door, I traverse in order courts, corridors, halls, and chapels; I see again the frescos and decorations; I find my way with ease through the labyrinth of the old castle to the moment of departure. But it is impossible for me to conceive of this imaginary visit as lasting two hours.

* Note again what happens when events are frequently repeated. I have made the journey from Paris to Brest a hundred times. All the images are superimposed, forming an indistinct mass; they are all, properly speaking, in the same vague state. Only those journeys marked by an important event appear as recollections; those alone which awaken secondary states of consciousness are localized in time, or remembered. It will be noted that our explanation of the mechanism of recollection corresponds with that given by Taine, *op. cit.*, second part, liv. i, ch. ii, § 6.

It seems much more brief, and the difference would be greater still if the same time had been occupied in some analogous way, or in agreeable company. If we declare the two periods to be equal, it is because we put our faith in a time-piece rather than in the testimony of consciousness.

All recollection, however clear it may be, undergoes an enormous contraction; this fact is indisputable and invariable. The law is confirmed by scientific experiments applied to very simple cases where the chances of error are very small. Vierordt has shown that if we endeavor to imagine fractions of a second, our idea of the given duration is always too large; the contrary is true when it is a question of several minutes or several hours. To study the duration of these small intervals he caused an assistant to observe for a certain time the beatings of a pendulum, and then to imitate them as closely as possible. The interval of the imitated series was always too long when the original interval was short, too short when the original was long. *

With complex states of consciousness, the error increases; and the problem is the more dif-

* Vierordt, "Der Zeitsinn nach Versuchen," 36–111. Analogous experiments by H. Weber on visual perceptions, "Tastsinn und Gemeingefühl," 87. See, also, Hermann's "Handbuch der Physiologie," 1879, v. ii, second part, p. 282.

ficult of exact solution since the contraction does not follow any appreciable law. We can not say that it is proportional to distance in time; indeed, we may assume the contrary. If I represent the past ten years of my life by a line one metre long, the last year would extend over three or four decimetres; the fifth, very eventful, would occupy two decimetres; and the other eight would be compressed into the remaining space.

In history the same illusion is noticeable. Certain centuries appear to be longer than others; and, if I am not mistaken, the period extending back from our day to the taking of Constantinople seems longer that that which extends from the last-named event to the First Crusade, although, chronologically speaking, the two are very nearly equal. This impression is probably due to the fact that the first is better known, and that our personal recollections are mingled with it.

In proportion as the present supplants the past, states of consciousness disappear and are effaced. After a short time but little remains; the greater part are veiled in an oblivion whence they never emerge, and they take with them the quantity of duration inherent in each; consequently, the elimination of states of consciousness is an elimination of time. Now, the abbreviated processes of which we have spoken suppose such elimination. If, to reach a distant recollection, it were necessary to traverse the entire series of intervening terms, memory would be impossible, because of the length of time required for the operation. *

We arrive, then, at this paradoxical conclusion: that one condition of memory is forgetfulness. Without the total obliteration of an immense number of states of consciousness, and the momentary repression of many more, recollection would be impossible. Forgetfulness, except in certain cases, is not a disease of memory, but a condition of health and life. We discover here a striking analogy with two essential vital processes. To live is to acquire and lose; life consists of dissolution as well as assimilation. Forgetfulness is dissolution.

Knowledge of the past (and here we are led back to the functions of vision) may also be compared to a picture of a distant landscape, at once deceptive and exact, since its very exacti-

* Abercrombie ("Inquiries Concerning the Intellectual Powers," p. 101) furnishes a proof: "The late Dr. Leyden was remarkable for his memory. I am informed, through a gentleman who was intimately acquainted with him, that he could repeat correctly a long act of Parliament, or any similar document, after having once read it. When he was, on one occasion, congratulated by a friend for his remarkable power in this respect, he replied that, instead of an advantage, it was often a source of great inconvenience. This he explained by saying that, when he wished to recollect a particular point in anything which he had read, he could do it only by repeating to himself the whole *from the commencement* till he reached the point which he wished to recall."

tude is derived from illusion. If we could compare our past, as it has really been, fixed before us objectively, with the subjective representation which we have in memory, we would find the copy formed upon a particular system of projection: each of us is able to find his way without trouble in this system, because he has himself created it.

IV.

Having thus traced the development of memory to its highest point, we will now follow the inverse order and return to the proposition from which we started. This return is necessary that we may show for the second time that memory consists of a variable process of organization between two extreme limits: a new state—organic registration. There is no form of mental activity more strongly in favor of the theory of evolution. From this point of view, and from this alone, are we able to comprehend the nature of memory; we see that its study is not only a physiology, but something more—a morphology—that is to say, a history of transformations.

Let us take up the subject, then, at the point at which we left it. A new acquisition of the mind, more or less complex, is revived for the first or second time. These recollections are the most unstable elements of memory—so unstable that many disappear for ever; such are the greater number of incidents coming daily within our observation. However clear and intense these recollections may be, they have a minimum of organization. But on each return, whether voluntary or involuntary, they gain in stability; the tendency to organization is accentuated.

Below this group of fully conscious and unorganized recollections we find another group, conscious and semi-organized — for example, a language that we are learning, a scientific theory or a manual art that we have only partly mastered. Here the distinctively individual character of the first group is effaced; recollection becomes more and more impersonal; it becomes objective. Localization in time disappears, because it is useless. Here and there isolated terms retain personal impressions which are localized. I remember having learned such a German or English word, in such a city, under such circumstances. This is a *survival*, the mark of an anterior state, an original imprint. Little by little it is effaced, and this term assumes the commonplace impersonal character of all the others.

This knowledge of a science, a language, or an art, becomes more and more persistent. It withdraws progressively from the psychical sphere and approaches nearer and nearer to the nature of an organic memory. Such, in the case of an adult, is the memory of his mother tongue.

Still lower, we come upon a completely organized and almost unconscious memory, such as that of an expert musician, of a workman who has mastered his trade, or of an accomplished ballet-dancer. And yet all this belongs, strictly speaking and in the ordinary meaning of the word, to a fully conscious memory.

We may go lower still. The exercise of each of our faculties (sight, touch, locomotion) implies a completely organized memory. But this is so much a part of our natural selves that few suspect with what difficulty it has been acquired. It is the same with a multitude of opinions in daily life. "No one remembers that the object at which he is looking has an opposite side; or that a certain modification of the visual impression implies a certain distance; or that a certain motion of the legs will move him forward; or that the thing which he sees moving about is a live animal. It would be thought a misuse of language were any one to ask another whether he *remembered* that the sun shines, that fire burns, that iron is hard, and that ice is cold." * And yet we repeat, all this in a nascent intelligence belongs to memory in the strictest sense.

It is not necessary to add that the preceding

* Spencer, "Principles of Psychology," part iv, ch. vi, § 192. This chapter is very important with regard to memory considered as a product of evolution.

is an ideal sketch, a scheme. It would be doubly illusory to endeavor to circumscribe clearly an evolution which takes place by insensible transitions, and which, moreover, varies with each individual.

Can we go farther? We can. Below the compound reflex impressions representing organic memory at its lowest term there are simple reflex impressions. These, resulting from innate anatomical conditions, have been acquired and fixed by long-continued experience in the evolution of species. We thus pass from individual to hereditary memory, which is a specific memory. It is enough to indicate this hypothesis.

In fact, we see that it is impossible to determine where memory—whether psychical or organic—ends. In what we designate under the collective name of memory there are series having every degree of organization, from a nascent state, to that which is most highly developed. There is an incessant transition from the unstable to the stable, from a state of consciousness with indeterminate acquisition to an organic state the acquisition fixed. Thanks to this continual movement toward organization, there is a simplification, an order, which leaves room for the highest form of thought. Left to itself, with no opposing forces, the process of registration would tend to the progressive destruction of consciousness, and would transform man into an automaton.

Suppose a human adult so situated that all new states of consciousness—perceptions, ideas, images, sentiments, desires — are not retained; then the series of conscious states constituting each form of psychical activity will in time become so well organized that all his acts will be entirely automatic. Shallow and commonplace minds realize this hypothesis to a certain extent. Confined to a narrow circle from which they exclude so far as possible all that is new or spontaneous, they tend toward a state of perfect stability; they become mere machines; for the greater portion of their lives consciousness is a superfluous factor.

Having considered our subject in all its bearings, we now return to the proposition with which we began: Conscious memory is only a particular phase of biological memory. We may, by another method, show once more that memory is attached to the fundamental conditions of life.

Every form of memory, from the highest to the lowest, is maintained by dynamical associations between nervous elements and particular modifications of these elements, or of their component cells. These modifications, resulting from a first impression, are not conserved in inert matter; they do not resemble the imprint of a seal upon wax. They are recorded in living matter. Now, living tissues are in a state of continuous molecular renovation, nervous tissue more than any other, and, in nervous tissue, the gray substance more than the white substance, as is shown by the excessive abundance of blood-vessels with which the former is lined. Since the modifications are persistent, the new material, the arrangement of the new molecules, must exactly reproduce the type which they replace. Memory depends directly upon nutrition.

But the cells have not only the power of self-nourishment. They are endowed, at least during a portion of life, with the faculty of reproduction, and we shall see farther on how this fact explains certain cases of restored memory. Physiologists are agreed that this reproduction is only one form of nutrition. The basis of memory is, therefore, nutrition; that is to say, the vital process *par excellence.*

I shall not now dwell upon this point. When we have spoken of the disorders of memory, its exaltation and depression, its momentary suspension and sudden return, and of its progressive impairment, we may recur to this part of our subject with profit; then the importance of nutrition will be self-evident.

Heretofore we have confined ourselves to preliminary study of memory in a state of health. We must now consider it in a morbid state. The pathology of memory completes its physiology; we shall see if it also confirms it.

CHAPTER II.

GENERAL AMNESIA.

MATERIALS for the study of the diseases of memory are abundant. They are scattered through books of medicine, works on mental disorders, and the writings of many psychologists. They may, with some little trouble, be brought together, and we have then at hand all the facts needed to facilitate investigation. The difficulty lies in classifying them; in giving to each case its proper interpretation; in learning its true bearing upon the mechanism of memory. In this respect, facts collected at random are very unequal in value; the most extraordinary are not the most instructive; the most curious are not the best sources of light. Physicians, to whom we owe them for the most part, have described and studied only from a professional stand-point. A disorder of memory is to them only a symptom, and is so recorded; it serves to establish a given diagnosis and prognosis. It is the same with classification: the observer is content with associating each case of amnesia with the morbid state of which it is the effect ; thus we have amnesia from softening of the brain, hemorrhage, cerebral disturbance, or intoxication.

From our point of view, however, diseases of memory must be studied by themselves, as morbid psychical states, through which we better understand the same elements in a healthy condition. As to classification, we are forced to arrange them according to external resemblances. Our knowledge of the subject is not sufficiently advanced to permit us to undertake a natural classification—that is, by causes. I may state now, to obviate further explanation, that the classification which follows is of value only as it serves to bring a degree of order into a confused and heterogeneous mass of facts, and that in many respects it is entirely arbitrary.

Certain diseases of memory may be limited to a single category of recollections, leaving the remainder apparently intact: these are partial disorders. Others, on the contrary, affect the entire memory in all its forms; completely dissever mental life; produce chasms that can never be bridged over; or demolish it altogether through long-continued activity: these are general disorders. We shall distinguish, then, in the first place, between two great classes—general diseases and partial diseases of memory. The former only will be considered in this chapter, and will be studied in the following order: 1. Temporary amnesia; 2. Periodical amnesia; 3. Progressive amnesia, the most curious and instructive of all; 4. In conclusion, a few words with regard to congenital amnesia.

I.

Temporary amnesia usually makes its appearance suddenly, and ends in the same way. It embraces periods of time which may vary from a few minutes to several years. The briefest, the clearest, and the most common forms are met with in cases of epilepsy. Physicians are not in accord with regard to the nature, the seat, or the causes of this malady. The solution of the problem is not within the scope or province of this work. It is enough for us to know that all authorities agree in recognizing three forms: grand mal, petit mal, and epileptic vertigo; that these are regarded less as distinct varieties than as different degrees of the same morbid state; and, lastly, that the more moderate the attack in external manifestations the more fatal it is to the mind. The attack is followed by a mental disorder which may reveal itself in odd or ridiculous acts or in crime. All of these acts have a common characteristic, designated by Dr. Hughlings Jackson as *mental automatism*. They leave no recollection save in a few instances, and then the traces of memory are very slight.

A patient while consulting with his physician is seized with epileptic vertigo. He soon recovers, but has forgotten having paid his fee a moment before the attack. An educated man, thirty-one years of age, found himself at his desk feeling rather confused, but not otherwise ill. He remembered having ordered his dinner, but not of eating or paying for it. He returned to the dining-room, learned that he had both eaten and paid, showing no signs of being ill, and had set out for his office. Unconsciousness lasted about three quarters of an hour. Another epileptic, seized with a sudden paroxysm, fell in a shop, got up, and, eluding the shopman and his friends, ran away, leaving his hat and order-book behind. He was discovered a quarter of a mile away, asking for his hat at all the shops, but not having recovered his senses, nor did he become conscious until he got to the railway ten minutes after.* Trousseau reports the case of a magistrate who, attending a meeting of a learned society in Paris, went out bare-headed, walked as far as the Quay, returned to his place and took part

* Hughlings Jackson, "West Riding Lunatic Asylum Reports," vol. v, p. 116, *et seq.*

in the discussions, with no knowledge of what he had done. Very often acts begun in the normal state are continued by the patient during the period of automatism, or words just read are commented upon. We have given illustrations in the preceding chapter. Nothing is so common in this disease as ineffectual attempts at suicide, of which no traces remain in the memory after the epileptic vertigo. It is the same with criminal attempts. A shoemaker, seized with epileptic mania on his wedding day, killed his father-in-law with a blow from his knife. Coming to himself at the end of several days, he had not the slightest consciousness of what had taken place.*

From these examples the reader will comprehend the nature of epileptic amnesia better than by any general description. A certain period of mental activity is as if it had never been; the patient knows of it only through the testimony of others or his own vague conjectures. Such is the fact. As to its psychological interpretation, there are two possible hypotheses. We may conclude, either that the period of mental automatism is not accompanied by consciousness, in which case the amnesia does not need explanation, as, nothing having been produced, nothing could be conserved or reproduced; or consciousness does exist, but in so weak a form that amnesia ensues. I be-

* See, also, Morel, "Traité des maladies mentales," p. 695.

lieve that the second hypothesis is the true one in the majority of cases.

In the first place, to restrict ourselves to reason alone, it is not easy to suppose that very complicated acts adapted to different ends are executed without some consciousness, however intermittent. Enlarge the power of habit as much as we will, the fact remains that, if in uniformity of action consciousness tends to disappear, where there is diversity it tends to positive development. But reasoning provides us only with possibilities; experience alone can decide. Now, there are facts which prove the existence of a certain consciousness, even in the many cases where the patient retains no recollection of the attack. Several epileptics, addressed during the crisis in a brusque way and with a tone of command, replied to questions briefly and in apparent pain. When the attack was ended they remembered neither what had been said to them nor their own replies. A child made to inhale the vapor of ether or ammonia, of which the odor was disagreeable, cried, angrily: "Go away, go away, go away!" and when the attack was over knew nothing of what had taken place. Sometimes epileptics were able with much effort to recollect experiences during the attack, especially toward its close. They were then like persons emerging from a painful dream. The principal circumstances of the attack had escaped them; they began by denying acts which were imputed to them; little by little they remembered a certain number of details which they seemed to have forgotten at first.*

If, in these cases, it is reasonable to believe that consciousness was present, we may also affirm its existence in many other instances. The application, however, is not general. The magistrate just mentioned was able to direct his movements in such a manner as to evade obstacles, carriages, and passers-by, which denotes a certain degree of consciousness. But in an analogous case, recorded by Dr. Hughlings Jackson, the patient was thrown down by an omnibus, and at another time narrowly escaped a fall into the Thames.

How, then, are we to explain amnesia in cases where consciousness is indicated? By the extreme weakness of the conscious state. A state of consciousness is fixed definitely by two circumstances—intensity and repetition; the latter is allied with the former, since repetition is a sum of intensities. Here there is neither intensity nor repetition. The mental disorder which follows the attack has been very accurately defined by Jackson as "an epileptic dream." One of his patients, aged nineteen, and little likely to dogmatize upon such a question, gave utterance to the same

* Trousseau, "Leçons cliniques," t. ii, p. 114. Falret, *loc. cit.*

expression. "Last time he had a fit and went to bed, and when in bed said: 'Wait a bit, Bill, I am coming.' He went down-stairs, he unbolted the doors, and he went out in his night-shirt. He came to himself just as he was stepping on the cold stones, and then his father touched him. He said that he had had a dream. 'It's all right, I have had a dream.' He went to bed, and had not been in bed for five minutes when he began again talking of Bill (an acquaintance in the volunteers), saying: 'You are in a great hurry to get your coat on.' His father went into his bedroom again, called his brother, and got the patient into bed." *

Thus we may find in the dream an indication of the mental state of epileptics. Dreams of which all remembrance immediately vanishes are very common. We awake in the night; the recollection of an interrupted dream is very distinct; in the morning not a trace remains. This is still more striking when we awake at the ordinary hour. The visions of the night are then very vivid, a short time elapses, and they are effaced for ever. Who has not lost himself in vain efforts to recall a dream of the preceding night, of which he remembers nothing, not even that it was a dream? The explanation is simple. The states of consciousness which constitute the dream are

* "West Riding Asylum Reports," vol. v, p. 124.

extremely weak. They seem to be strong, not because they are so in reality, but because no other stronger state exists to force them into a secondary position. From the moment of awakening the conditions change. Images disappear before perceptions, perceptions before a state of sustained attention, a state of sustained attention before a fixed idea. In fact, consciousness during the majority of dreams is at a minimum of intensity.

The difficulty is in explaining why, in the period following the epileptic attack, consciousness falls to a minimum. Neither physiology nor psychology is able to solve the problem, since each ignores the conditions of the genesis of consciousness. The question is the more difficult when amnesia is allied with epileptic delirium, and with it alone. Note, for instance, what happens when the subject is at once the victim of alcoholism and epilepsy. A patient is seized during the day with an epileptic attack, breaks everything within his reach, and conducts himself with great violence. After a brief period of respite he is seized in the night with alcoholic delirium, characterized by the usual terrifying visions. The next day, on coming to himself, he remembers the delirium of the night; but of the delirium of the day no recollection remains.*

* Magnan, "Clinique de Sainte-Anne," March 3, 1879.

There is another difficulty. If amnesia arises from weakness in the primitive states of consciousness, how is it that these states, hypothetically weak, inspire determinate acts? According to Jackson, there is during the paroxysm an internal discharge sufficient to incapacitate the highest nervous centers. "Mental automatism results . . . from over-action of low nervous centers, because the highest or controlling centers have been thus put out of use." * We have here only a special application of a well-known physiological law: The excito-motor power of reflex centers increases when their connection with the superior centers is destroyed. †

We may limit ourselves to the psychological problem. If we insist upon regarding consciousness as a "force," existing and acting by itself, no explanation is possible. But if we admit, as was said in the preceding chapter, that consciousness is the accompaniment of a nervous state which remains the fundamental element, the matter is clear. At least, there is no contradiction in admitting that a nervous state, suf-

* "West Riding Asylum Reports," vol. v, p. 111.

† A very important characteristic of epileptic mania, says Falret (*loc. cit.*), is the absolute resemblance of all attacks in the same patient, not only in general, but in the smallest detail. The same patient expresses the same ideas, utters the same words, performs the same acts. There is a surprising uniformity in the different attacks.

ficient to determine certain acts, may be insufficient to awaken consciousness. The production of a movement and that of a state of consciousness are two distinct and independent facts; the conditions of existence of the one are not those of the other. Let us note in closing that the fatal consequence of repeated epileptic seizures, especially in the form of vertigo, is the progressive and final destruction of memory. This phase of amnesia will be studied in another place.

We pass now to cases of temporary amnesia of a destructive character. In the cases just given the capital accumulated up to the development of the disease was not lost; it simply happened that something which had been in the consciousness no longer remained in the memory. In the cases which follow, a part of the capital is lost. These cases afford a rich field of interest, and it is possible that one day, with further progress in the applications of physiology and psychology, we may learn much from them concerning the nature of memory. In the present stage of knowledge they are not the most instructive—at least in my judgment, and I say this with no desire to underrate their value to others.

These cases differ very much one from another. Sometimes the suspension of memory begins with the disease and extends forward; sometimes it extends backward over events recently past; oftener it extends in both directions. Sometimes memory returns of itself and suddenly; sometimes slowly and with assistance; sometimes the loss is absolute, and complete reeducation is necessary. We shall give examples of each.

"A young woman, married to a man whom she loved passionately, was seized during confinement with prolonged syncope, at the end of which she lost all recollection of events that had occurred since her marriage, inclusive of that ceremony. She remembered very clearly the rest of her life up to that point. . . . At first she pushed her husband and child from her with evident alarm. She has never recovered recollection of this period of her life, nor of any of the impressions received during that time. Her parents and friends have convinced her that she is married and has a son. She believes their testimony, because she would rather think that she has lost a year of her life than that all her associates are impostors. But conviction and consciousness are not united. She looks upon husband and child without being able to realize how she gained the one and gave birth to the other." *

* "Lettre de Charles Villiers à G. Cuvier" (Paris: Lenor-

Here we have an example of incurable amnesia, extending only into the past. As to psychological courses, they may be found in the destruction of residua and the impossibility of their reproduction. In other cases amnesia extends forward, and is therefore to be attributed to the impossibility of registration and conservation of succeeding states of consciousness.

Generally, in cases of temporary amnesia resulting from cerebral shock, there is a retroactive effect. The patient, on recovering consciousness, is found to have lost not only all recollection of the accident and the period following, but also of a more or less extended time anterior to that event. Many examples might be given; I shall cite only one, recorded by Carpenter.

A Mr. H. "was driving his wife and child in a phaeton, when the horse took fright and ran away; and, all attempts to pull him in being unsuccessful, the phaeton was at last violently dashed against a wall, and Mr. H. was thrown out, sustaining a severe concussion of the brain. On recovering, he found that he had forgotten the *immediate* antecedents of the accident, the

mant, 1802), cited by L. Villermay, "Essais sur les maladies de la mémoire," pp. 76, 77. This little work, otherwise of small value, appeared in the "Mémoires" of the Paris Société de Médecine, 1817, vol. i.

last thing he remembered being that he had met an acquaintance on the road about two miles from the scene of it. Of the efforts he had made, and the terror of his wife and child, he has not, to this day, any recollection whatever."*

We come now to cases of amnesia much more grave in character, in several instances requiring complete re-education. The following are taken from the English review, "Brain":

The first case, reported by Dr. J. Mortimer Granville, is that of a young woman, aged twenty-six, hysterical and choreic, who, after a paroxysm of considerable violence, fell into a state verging on suspended animation.

"When consciousness began to return, the latest sane ideas formed previous to the illness mingled curiously with the new impressions received, as in the case of a person awakening slowly from a dream. When propped up with pillows in bed near the window, so that passers in the street could be seen, the patient described the moving objects as 'trees walking'; and when asked where she saw these things, she invariably replied 'in the other Gospel.' In short, her mental state was one in which the real and ideal were not separable. Her recollections on recovery, and

* *Op. cit.*, p. 450.

for some time afterward, were indistinct, and, in regard to a large class of common topics which must have formed the staple material of thought up to the period of the attack, memory was blank. Special subjects of thought immediately anterior to the malady seemed to have saturated the mind so completely that the early impressions received after recovery commenced were imbued with them, while the cerebral record of penultimate brain-work in the life before the morbid state was, as it were, obliterated. For example, although this young woman had supported herself by daily duty as a governess, she had no recollection of so simple a matter as the use of a writing implement. When a pen or pencil was placed in her hand, as it might be thrust between the fingers of a child, the act of grasping it was not excited, even reflexly; the touch or sight of the instrument awoke no association of ideas. The most perfect destruction of brain-tissue could not have more completely effaced the constructive effect of education and habit on the cerebral elements. This state lasted some weeks." * Recovery of the memory was slow and painful, requiring a process of re-education as distinct as that in the case which follows.

This, reported by Professor William Sharpey,

* "Brain: A Journal of Neurology," October, 1879, p. 317, *et seq.*

is one of the most curious instances of re-education on record. We give only the psychological details. The patient was a young married woman, about twenty-four years of age, of pale complexion and slender make, who, for about six weeks, remained in a continuous state of somnolence, the torpor increasing from day to day until finally (about the 10th of June) it became impossible to rouse her. She remained in this condition for nearly two months. When food was presented to her lips with a spoon, she readily took it into her mouth and swallowed it; when satisfied, she closed her teeth to signify the fact, and, if importuned to take more, turned away her mouth. She seemed to distinguish different flavors, for she manifested an evident preference for some sorts of food and obstinately refused others. She had occasional intervals of waking at uncertain and distant periods. She answered no question, and recognized nobody "except one old acquaintance, whom she had not seen for more than twelve months. She looked steadfastly in this person's face for a few seconds, apparently occupied in trying to remember his name, which at length she found out and repeated again and again, at the same time taking him by the hand as if overjoyed to see him." She then fell again into slumber. Toward the end of August she returned, little by little, to a normal condition. Here began the work of re-education.

"On her recovery from the torpor, she appeared to have forgotten nearly all her previous knowledge; everything seemed new to her, and she did not recognize a single individual—not even her nearest relatives. In her behavior she was restless and inattentive, but very lively and cheerful; she was delighted with everything she saw or heard, and altogether resembled a child more than a grown person.

"In a short time she became more sedate, and her attention could be longer fixed on one object. Her memory, too, so entirely lost as far as regarded previous knowledge, was soon found to be most acute and retentive with respect to everything she saw or heard subsequently to her disorder; and she has by this time recovered many of her former acquirements, some with greater, others with less facility. With regard to these, it is remarkable that though the process followed in regaining many of them apparently consisted in recalling them to mind with the assistance of her neighbors, rather than in studying them anew, yet even now she does not appear to be in the smallest degree conscious of having possessed them before.

"At first it was scarcely possible to engage her in conversation; in place of answering a question, she repeated it aloud in the same words in which it was put, and even long after she came to answer questions she constantly repeated them once over before giving her reply. At first she had very few words, but she soon acquired a great many, and often strangely misapplied them. She did this, however, for the most part in particular ways; she often, for instance, made one word answer for all others which were in any way allied to it; thus, in place of 'tea,' she would ask for 'juice,' and this word she long used for liquids. For a long time, also, in expressing the qualities of objects, she invariably, where it was possible, used the words denoting the very opposite of what she intended, and thus she would say 'white' in place of 'black,' 'hot' for 'cold,' etc. She would often also talk of her arm when she meant her leg, her eye when she meant her tooth, etc. She now generally uses her words with propriety, although she is sometimes apt to change their terminations, or compose new ones of her own.

"She has as yet recognized no person, not even her nearest connections; that is to say, she has no recollection of having seen or known them previously to her illness, though she is aware of having seen them since, and calls them either by their right names or by those of her own giving; but she knows them only as new acquaintances, and has no idea of what relation they sustain to herself. She has not seen above a dozen people since her illness, and she looks on these as all that she has ever known.

"Among other acquirements she has recovered that of reading; but it was requisite to begin her with the alphabet, as she at first did not know a single letter. She afterward learned to form syllables and small words, and now she reads tolerably well, and has shown herself much interested in several stories previously unknown to her, which she has read since her recovery. The reacquisition of her reading was eventually facilitated by singing the words of familiar songs, from the printed page, while she played on the piano. In learning to write she began with the most elementary lessons, but made much more rapid progress than a person who had never before been taught. Very soon after the torpor left her she could sing many of her old songs, and play on the piano-forte with little or no assistance, and she has since continued to practice her music, which now affords her great pleasure and amusement. In singing, she at first generally required to be helped to the first two or three words of a line, and made out the rest apparently from memory. She can play from the music-book several tunes which she had never seen before; and her friends are inclined to think that she now plays and sings fully as well, if not better, than she did previously to her illness. She learned backgammon, which she formerly knew, and several games at cards, with very little trouble; and she can now knit worsted, and do several other sorts of work; but with regard to all these acquirements, as already mentioned, it is remarkable that she appears not to have the slightest remembrance of having possessed them before, although it is plain that the process of recovery has been greatly aided by previous knowledge, which, however, she seems unconscious of having ever acquired. When asked how she had learned to play the notes of music from a book, she replied that she could not tell, and only wondered why her questioner could not do the same.

"She has once or twice had dreams, which she afterward related to her friends, and she seemed quite aware of the difference betwixt a dream and a reality; indeed, from several casual remarks which she makes of her own accord, it would appear that she possesses many general ideas of a more or less complex nature, which she has had no opportunity of acquiring since her recovery." *

So far as we can judge from Professor Sharpey's report, re-education lasted in this instance

* "Brain," April, 1879, p. 1, *et seq.*

only about three months. The case, moreover, is by no means unique:

"A clergyman, of rare talent and energy, of sound education, was thrown from his carriage and received a violent concussion of the brain. For several days he remained utterly unconscious, and when restored his intellect was observed to be in a state similar to that of a naturally intelligent child. Although in middle life, he commenced his English and classical studies under tutors, and was progressing satisfactorily, when, after several months' successful study, his memory gradually returned, and his mind resumed all its wonted vigor and its former wealth and polish of culture."*

"A gentleman about thirty years of age, of learning and acquirements, at the termination of a severe illness was found to have lost the recollection of everything, even the names of the most common objects. His health being restored, ho began to re-acquire knowledge like a child. After learning the names of objects, he was taught to read, and, after this, began to learn Latin. He made considerable progress, when, one day, in reading his lesson with his brother, who was his teacher, he suddenly stopped and put his hand to his head. Being asked why he did so, he replied: 'I feel a peculiar sensation

* Forbes Winslow, *op. cit.*, p. 317.

in my head; and now it appears to me that I knew all this before.' From that time he rapidly recovered his faculties." *

I am content for the moment to bring these facts to the attention of the reader. Any comments which they may suggest will find a more appropriate place elsewhere. I will close with a case little known, and which forms a natural transition to the group of intermittent amnesia. We see, in fact, a provisional memory gradually formed, only to disappear suddenly before the primitive memory.

A young woman, of robust constitution and good health, accidentally fell into a river and was nearly drowned. For six hours she was insensible, but then returned to consciousness. Ten days later she was seized with a stupor which lasted for four hours. When she opened her eyes she failed to recognize her friends, and was utterly deprived of the senses of hearing, taste, and smell, as well as the power of speech. There remained to her only the senses of sight and touch, which were both abnormally sensitive. She was apparently quite lost to everything that went on about her, and, like an animal deprived of its brain, remained in any position in which she was placed. Her appetite was good, but she ate indifferently, in a perfectly automatic man-

* Forbes Winslow, *op. cit.*, p. 317.

ner. So automatic was her life that for days her sole occupation was in pulling or cutting various objects into pieces of great minuteness, such as flowers, articles of clothing, waste paper, an old straw bonnet, etc. Later, she was supplied with materials for patchwork, and, after some initiatory instruction, she took her needle and labored incessantly from morning to night, making no distinction between Sundays and weekdays, since she could not be made to comprehend the difference. She had no remembrance from day to day of what she had been doing the previous day, and so every morning commenced *de novo.* She gradually, however, began, like a child, to register ideas and acquire experience. She was then led to the higher art of worsted work. She was delighted with the colors and the flowers upon the patterns, and seemed to derive special pleasure from the harmony of tints. But every day she began something new, unless her unfinished work was placed before her, forgetting what had been done the day before.

The first ideas derived from her former experience, that seemed to be awakened within her, were connected with two subjects which had naturally made a strong impression upon her—namely, her fall into the river, and a love affair. When she was shown a landscape in which there was a river, or the view of a troubled sea, she became intensely agitated, and one of her attacks of spasmodic rigidity and insensibility immediately followed. So great was her feeling of fright associated with water that she trembled at the mere sight of it running from one vessel to another. When she washed her hands they were merely placed in water without rubbing them together.

From an early stage of her illness she derived obvious pleasure from the visits of a young man to whom she had been attached; he was evidently an object of interest when nothing else would rouse her. He came regularly every evening, and she as regularly looked for his coming. At a time when she did not remember from one hour to another what she was doing, she would look anxiously for the opening of the door about the time he was accustomed to pay her a visit; and, if he did not come, she was fretful throughout the entire evening. When, by her removal into the country, she lost sight of him for a time, she became unhappy and irritable, and suffered frequently from attacks of spasmodic rigidity and insensibility. When, on the other hand, he remained near her there was a progressive return of the intellectual powers and memory.

This return was, however, gradually going on. One day, seeing her mother in a state of grief, she suddenly cried out, with some hesitation, "What's the matter?" From this time she began to articulate a few words; but she neither called persons nor things by their right names. The pronoun "this" was her favorite word; and it was applied alike to every individual object, animate and inanimate. The first objects which she called by their right names were wild flowers, for which she had shown quite a passion when a child; and at this time she had not the least recollection of the friends and places of her childhood.

"The mode of recovery of this patient was quite as remarkable as anything in her history. Her health and bodily strength seemed completely re-established, her vocabulary was being extended, and her mental capacity was improving, when she became aware that her lover was paying attention to another woman. This idea immediately and very naturally excited the emotion of jealousy; which, if we analyze it, will appear to be nothing else than a painful feeling connected with the idea of the faithlessness of the object beloved. On one occasion this feeling was so strongly excited that she fell down in a fit of insensibility, which resembled her first attack in duration and severity. This, however, proved sanatory. When the insensibility passed off, she was no longer spell-bound. The veil of oblivion was withdrawn; and, as if awakening from a sleep of twelve months' duration, she found herself surrounded by her grandfather, grandmother, and their familiar friends and acquaintances, in the old house at Shoreham. She awoke in the possession of her natural faculties and former knowledge, but without the slightest remembrance of anything which had taken place in the year's interval, from the invasion of the first fit up to present time. She spoke, but she heard not; she was still deaf, but, being able to read and write as formerly, she was no longer cut off from association with others. From this time she rapidly improved, but for some time continued deaf. She soon perfectly understood by the motion of her lips what her mother said; they conversed with facility and quickness together, but she did not understand the language of the lips of a stranger. She was completely unaware of the change in her lover's affections, which had taken place in her state of 'second consciousness'; and a painful explanation was necessary. This, however, she bore very well; and she has since recovered her previous bodily and mental health." *

We shall see later on, after the various facts to be considered are disposed of, what general conclusions with regard to the mechanism of memory

* Dunn, in the "Lancet," November 15 and 29, 1845. *Vide* Carpenter, *op. cit.*, p. 460, *et seq.*

are to be derived from its pathology. For the moment, we limit ourselves to a few remarks suggested by the preceding cases. It is first to be observed that these, although grouped indiscriminately by medical authorities under the general head of total amnesia, belong, in fact, from a psychological point of view, to two distinct morbid types. The first type (represented by the cases cited by Villiers and Granville) is by far the most frequent. If we have given but few examples, it is because we would not weary the reader with monotonous and unprofitable repetitions. It is characterized psychologically by the fact that amnesia appears only in the less automatic and less organized phases of memory. In cases belonging to this morbid group neither habits, nor aptitude for mechanical work, such as that of sewing or embroidery, nor the faculty of reading, writing, or speaking a native or foreign language, is in the least affected; in a word, memory, in its organized or semi-organized form, remains intact. Pathological destruction is limited to the most highly developed and most unstable forms of memory, to those which have a personal character, and which, accompanied by consciousness and localization in time, constitute what we denominated in the preceding chapter the psychical memory, properly so called. Moreover, it must be observed that amnesia affects the most recent events, extending backward over a period of variable duration.* At first thought, this fact is surprising, since our latest recollections are apparently the most vivid, the strongest, of all. In truth, it is logical, the stability of any recollection being in direct ratio with its degree of organization. But this point will be considered farther on.

The physiological cause of amnesia in this group is only amenable to hypothesis; probably it varies with each case. At first, the faculty for registering new impressions is temporarily suspended; as they appear, states of consciousness vanish and leave no trace. But preceding recollections, registered for weeks, months, years—where are they? They have long endured, they have been conserved and frequently reproduced, they seemed to be a stable acquisition, and yet their place is a blank. The patient is able to regain them only indirectly and by artifice—the testimony of others or his personal reflections which unite the present in a more or less imperfect fashion with what remains of his past. Observation does not show that this chasm is ever bridged by direct recollection. Thus two

* I must mention in passing an incident reported by Brown-Séquard of a patient who, after an attack of apoplexy, lost all recollection of five years of his life. These five years, which comprised the period of his marriage, ended just six months before the date of the attack.

suppositions are possible: either the registration of anterior states is effaced, or, the conservation of anterior states persisting, their power of revivification by association with the present is destroyed. It is impossible to decide arbitrarily between these two hypotheses.

The second morbid type is less frequent, and is represented by the cases cited by Sharpey and Winslow (that of Dunn forms a transition to the group classed as intermittent amnesia). Here the work of destruction is complete; memory in all its forms—organized, semi-organized, or conscious—is totally suppressed; amnesia is complete. We have seen that writers who have described the disease in this form compare the patient to an infant and his mind with a *tabula rasa*. These expressions, however, are not to be taken too literally. The instance of re-education recorded above shows that, if all anterior experience is wiped out, certain latent aptitudes still remain in the brain. The extreme rapidity of re-education, especially toward the last, can not be otherwise explained. Facts indubitably show that this return of knowledge which appears to be the work of art is really the work of nature. Memory returns because the atrophied nervous elements are supplanted in time by other elements having the same properties, primitive and acquired, as those which they replace. This again demonstrates the relation existing between memory and nutrition.

Finally—for all observations upon amnesia can not be reduced to a single formula—in cases where the loss and return of memory are sudden we recognize an analogy with the phenomena of arrested functions or "inhibition," a subject to which physiologists have given much study and concerning which very little is known. These points are indicated by way of illustration. An extended analysis at this stage would be premature. Let us continue our review of recorded facts with a consideration of periodic amnesia.

II.

The study of amnesia in its periodic form is better calculated to throw light upon the nature of the *Ego* and the conditions for the existence of a conscious personality than to exhibit the mechanism of memory from a new stand-point. It forms an interesting chapter in a work as yet incomplete, and which might be properly entitled "Diseases and Aberrations of the Personality." It will be difficult for us to avoid the subject, since it confronts us on every side. But I shall endeavor to say only what is indispensable to clearness of exposition. I shall be sparing of illustrations; they are sufficiently familiar, the study of the so-called phenomena of "double consciousness" being a common pastime. The detailed and instructive observations of Dr. Azam in particular have contributed largely to the popular knowledge of periodic amnesia. I shall limit myself, then, to a review of important cases, taking up first the manifestations of periodic amnesia in its most highly developed form, and proceeding to those of a less complicated nature.

I. The most clearly defined and the most complete instance of periodic amnesia on record is the case of a young American woman reported by Macnish in his "Philosophy of Sleep";* it has been often quoted:

"Her memory was capacious and well stored with a copious stock of ideas. Unexpectedly, and without any forewarning, she fell into a profound sleep, which continued several hours beyond the ordinary term. On waking, she was discovered to have lost every trace of acquired knowledge. Her memory was *tabula rasa*—all vestiges, both of words and things, were obliterated and gone. It was found necessary for her to learn everything again. She even acquired, by new efforts, the art of spelling, reading, writing, and calculating, and gradually became acquainted with the persons and objects around, like a being for the first time brought into the

* Page 167.

world. In these exercises she made considerable proficiency. But, after a few months, another fit of somnolency invaded her. On rousing from it, she found herself restored to the state she was in before the first paroxysm; but was wholly ignorant of every event and occurrence that had befallen her afterward. The former condition of her existence she now calls the old state, and the latter the new state; and she is as unconscious of her double character as two distinct persons are of their respective natures. For example, in her old state she possesses all the original knowledge, in her new state only what she acquired since. . . . In the old state she possesses fine powers of penmanship, while in the new she writes a poor, awkward hand, having not had time or means to become an expert." These periodical transitions lasted for four years.

Setting aside for the moment all that concerns the alternation of two personalities, it should be noted that there were formed here two memories, each complete and absolutely independent of the other. Not only was the memory of personal impressions, the memory of consciousness, entirely and hopelessly dissevered, but also the semi-organic, semi-conscious memory by which we are able to speak, to read, and to write. The record does not tell us whether or no this disruption of memory extended to its purely organic forms—to habits (whether, for instance, the patient was obliged to learn anew the use of the hands in eating, dressing, etc.). But, even supposing that this group of acquisitions remained intact, the separation into two distinct and independent groups is still as complete as the most exacting observer could desire.

Dr. Azam records a case similar to the preceding, although not so clearly manifested. The normal memory disappeared and reappeared periodically. In the abnormal interval a new memory was not formed, but the patient retained faint traces of the primitive states. This, at least, is the inference from an observation whose psychological details are not always given with precision.* The subject was a young man who, after successive attacks of chorea, lost completely all memory of the past, forgot everything that had been taught him, could neither read, write, nor count, and did not recognize any of his attendants, with the exception of his father and mother and the Sister of Charity who acted as nurse. But while the amnesia lasted (the ordinary period was a month) the youth was able to

* "Revue Scientifique," December 22, 1877. The author says, for instance, that during one of the attacks the patient "conversed with intelligence and vivacity, without having recovered his memory"!

mount his horse, drive a carriage, follow the regular daily routine, and say his prayers at the proper time. Usually the return of memory was very sudden. So far as we can judge, there was a periodical suspension of memory in its unstable and partly stable, or — if the reader prefer — its conscious and semi-conscious, forms —consciousness being, in general, in inverse ratio to stability. But the organized, instinctive memory was not impaired; the last strongholds were not carried. I shall not dwell, however, upon the record of a case too deficient in psychological interpretation to be of much value.

II. A second, less complete but more common, form of periodic amnesia is that of which Dr. Azam gives an interesting description in the case of Félida X., and of which Dr. Dufay found a parallel in one of his own patients. The original records may be easily consulted, and a brief summary will suffice for our purpose.

A woman of hysterical temperament was attacked in 1856 with a singular malady affecting her in such a manner that she lived a double life, passing alternately from one to the other of two states which Dr. Azam defines as "the first condition" and "the second condition." In the normal, or first condition, the woman was serious, grave, reserved, and laborious. Suddenly, overcome with sleep, she would lose consciousness and awake in the second condition. In this state her character was changed; she became gay, imaginative, vivacious, and coquettish. "She remembered perfectly all that had taken place in other similar states and *during her normal life.*" Then, after the lapse of a longer or shorter period, she was again seized with a trance. On awaking she was in the first condition. But in this state she had no recollection of what had occurred in the second condition; she remembered only anterior normal periods. With increasing years the normal state (first condition) lasted for shorter and shorter and less frequent periods, while the transition from one state to the other, which had formerly occupied something like ten minutes, took place almost instantaneously.

Such are the essential facts in this case. For purposes of special study, it may be summed up in a few words. The patient passed alternately through two states; in one she possessed her memory entire; in the other she had only a partial memory formed of all the impressions received in that state.

The case reported by Dr. Dufay is analogous to that just given. During the period corresponding with the second condition of Félida X., the patient was able to recall the minutest incidents which had taken place in the normal state or during the period of somnambulism. There was also a change in character, and, during the period of complete memory, the patient designated the normal condition as "*d'état bête*"—the "brute state." *

It is worth noting that in this form of periodic amnesia there is a part of the memory which is never wiped out, but which remains common to both conditions. "In these two states," Dr. Azam tells us, "the patient was perfectly able to read, write, count, cut, and sew." There was not here, as in the case recorded by Macnish, complete disruption. The semi-conscious forms of memory co-operated equally with both phases of mental activity.

III. Our exposition of the different phases of periodic amnesia may be profitably concluded with the enumeration of certain cases in which they appear in an undeveloped form; they are met with in victims of somnambulism, whether natural or induced. Usually, somnambulists, after the attack, have no recollection of what they have done; but in each crisis there is recollection of preceding crises. There are exceptions to this law; but they are rare. The case, recorded by Macario, of a girl who was violated during one

* For further details, see Azam, "Revue Scientifique," 1867, May 20, September 16; 1877, November 10; 1879, March 8. And Dufay, *ibid.*, 1876, July 15.

attack, retaining no remembrance of it on awakening, but revealing the fact to her mother in a succeeding crisis, has been often cited. Dr. Mesnet was witness to an attempt at suicide begun in one and continued in the other of two consecutive attacks.* A young servant-maid believed herself every night to be a bishop, and spoke and acted consistently with that idea (Combe); and Hamilton speaks of a poor apprentice who, on going to sleep, imagined that he was the father of a family, wealthy, a senator, taking up the *rôle* every night and acting it in the most graphic manner, denying his real condition if any allusion was made to the subject in his presence. It is useless to multiply examples, as they may be found on every hand; the evident conclusion is that, side by side with the normal memory, there is formed during the attacks a partial, temporary, and parasitic memory.

On examining the general characteristics of periodic amnesia as illustrated in the cases given, we find, first, *an evolution of two memories*. In extreme cases (Macnish) the two memories are independent of one another; when one appears, the other disappears. Each is self-supporting; each utilizes, so to speak, its own material. The organized memory employed in speaking, reading, and writing is not a common basis of the two

* "Archives générales de médecine," 1860, v. xv, p. 147.

states. In each there is a distinct recollection of words, graphic signs, and the movements necessary to record them. In modified cases (Azam, Dufay, somnambulism) a partial memory alternates with the normal memory. The latter embraces the totality of conscious states; the former, a limited group of states which, by a natural process of selection, separate from the others, and form in the life of the individual a series of connected fragments. But they retain a common basis in the less stable and less conscious forms of memory which enter indifferently into either group.

As a result of this discerption of memory, the individual appears—at least to others—to be living a double life. The illusion is natural, the *Ego* depending (or appearing to depend) upon the possibility of association of present states with those that are reanimated or localized in the past, according to laws already formulated. There are here two distinct centers of association and attraction. Each draws to itself certain groups, and is without influence upon others. It is evident that this formation of two memories, entirely or partly independent of one another, is not a primitive cause; it is the symptom of a morbid process, the psychical expression of a disorder yet to be analyzed. And this leads us to a great subject, much to our regret, since we must treat it as a side issue: we refer to the conditions of personality.

Let us first reject the idea of an *Ego* conceived as a distinct entity of conscious states. Such an hypothesis is useless and contradictory; it is a conception worthy of a psychology in its infancy, content to accept superficial observations as the whole of truth and to theorize where it can not explain. I avow allegiance to contemporary science which sees in conscious personality a compound resultant of very complex states.

The *Ego* subjectively considered consists of a sum of conscious states. There is a central group surrounded by secondary states which tend to supplant it, and these in turn are encompassed in a similar manner with other less conscious states. The highest state, after a more or less extended period of vitality, succumbs, and is replaced by another, about which the remaining states group themselves as before. The mechanism of consciousness is comparable to that of vision. Here we have a visual point in which alone perception is clear and precise; about it is the visual field in which perception is progressively less clear and precise as we advance from center to circumference. The *Ego*, its present perpetually renewed, is for the most part nourished by the memory; that is to say, the present state is associated with others which, thrown back and localized in the past, constitute at each moment what we regard as our personality. In brief, the *Ego* may be considered in two ways: either in its actual form, and then it is the sum of existing conscious states; or, in its continuity with the past, and then it is formed by the memory according to the process outlined above.

It would seem, according to this view, that the identity of the *Ego* depended entirely upon the memory. But such a conception is only partial. Beneath the unstable compound phenomenon in all its protean phases of growth, degeneration, and reproduction, there is a something that remains: and this something is the undefined consciousness, the product of all the vital processes, constituting bodily perception, and which is expressed in one word—the *cœnæsthesis.** Our conception of this organic consciousness is so vague that it is difficult to speak of it in precise terms. It is a bodily condition which, perpetually renewed, is no more recognized than a habit. But although it is felt neither in

* The general feeling of well-being which results from a healthy condition of all the organs of the body, which is, indeed, the expression of a favorably proceeding organic life, is known as the *cœnæsthesis*, and is sometimes described as an emotion; but it is not truly an emotion; it is the body's sensation or feeling of its well-being, and marks a condition of things, therefore, in which activity of any kind will be pleasurable.—Maudsley, *op. cit.*, p. 135. [Tr.]

and of itself, nor in the gradual variations which mark its normal state, it passes through instantaneous or rapid modifications that produce radical changes in the personality. All observers are agreed that the early development of mental disease is indicated, not by intellectual disorder, but by changes in *character*—changes which are only the psychical expression of the cœnæsthesis. So an organic lesion, often ignored, may transform the cœnæsthesis, substituting for the normal sensation of existence a condition of melancholy, mental distress, and anxiety, of which the patient is unable to discern the cause; or, on the other hand, producing undue joyousness, exuberant emotions, and extreme content—misleading expressions of grave disorganization, of which the most striking example is seen in the euphrasia of the dying. Each of these changes has a physiological cause; together they represent the echoes of consciousness, and it is as reasonable to say that our every-day existence is not a mode of living because it is monotonous, as to say that these variations are felt, and that the normal state is imperceptible. This bodily condition, which is without the sphere of consciousness because of its perpetuity, is the true basis of personality—ever-present, ever-acting, without repose or respite, it knows neither sleep nor exhaustion, lasting as long as life itself, of which, indeed, it is only an expression. This it is that serves as support for the conscious *Ego* formed by the memory; it renders associations possible, and maintains them after they are formed.

The unity of the *Ego* is, then, not that of a mathematical point, but that of a very complicated mechanism. It is a consensus of vital processes, co-ordinated first by the nervous system —the chief regulator in the bodily economy—and finally by consciousness whose natural form is unity. It is, in fact, inherent in the nature of psychical states that they can co-exist only in a very limited number, grouped about a center which alone represents consciousness in the plenitude of its powers.

Suppose, now, that we are able at a single stroke to change the body and put another in its place—skeleton, vessels, viscera, muscles, integument all new—the nervous system alone, with all its past registered within, remaining intact. There can be no doubt that, in the efflux of unwonted vital sensations, the greatest disorder would arise. Between the primitive cœnæsthesis represented by the nervous system and the new cœnæsthesis acting with all the intensity of juvenescence, there would be an irreconcilable antagonism. This hypothesis is actually realized to a certain extent in morbid cases. Anæsthesia resulting from organic lesion sometimes modifies the cœnæsthesis to such a degree that the subject fancies himself made of stone, butter, wax, wood, to be changed in sex, or to be dead. Aside from such morbid cases, note what takes place at puberty. "When new organs come into action, after a primitive period of quiescence, with the total revolution produced in the organism, innumerable sensations, new desires, vague or distinct ideas, and novel impulses pass into the consciousness in a very brief space of time. Little by little they penetrate to the circle of primitive ideas, and finally become an integral part of the *Ego*—which by the same token is completely transformed; it is renewed, and the sentiment of personality undergoes a radical metamorphosis. Until assimilation is complete, this penetration and disintegration of the primitive *Ego* is accompanied by extreme commotion in the consciousness, which is the subject of the most tumultuous disturbance." * It may be said that whenever the changes in the cœnæsthesis, in place of being insensible or temporary, are rapid and permanent, there is discord between the two elements that constitute personality in its normal state: bodily sensation and conscious memory. If the new center holds its own, it becomes the point about which other new associa-

* Griesinger, "Traité des maladies mentales," p. 55, *et seq.* The entire passage is an excellent analysis.

tions are formed; and thus a new complexus, a new *Ego*, is developed. The antagonism between the two centers of attraction—the old, which is in the stage of dissolution, and the new, which is in the stage of evolution—produces results which vary with circumstances. Sometimes the primitive *Ego* disappears after enriching the new with the spoils of its accumulated wealth—that is to say, with a part of its constituent associations. Sometimes the two *Egos* alternate, neither being able to supplant the other. Sometimes the primitive *Ego* exists only in the memory; but, unconnected with any cœnæsthesis, appears to the new *Ego* as an extraneous entity.*

The preceding digression has been made to demonstrate what has already been affirmed—i. e., that periodic amnesia is only a secondary phenomenon; it has its origin in vital disorder—the sentiment of existence which is, properly speaking, only the sentiment of bodily unity, passing through two alternate phases. This is the primitive cause of the formation of two centers of association, and, consequently, of two memories.

* I thus explain a case recorded by Leuret ("Fragments psych. sur la folie," p. 277), often cited. A maniac, who always designated herself as "*la personne de moi-même*," had retained very clearly recollection of her life up to the beginning of her insanity; but she assigned this period to another. Of the primitive *Ego* only the memory remained. These disorders of personality are full of interest, but they are not within the province of our discussion.

If we continue our inquiry, other questions arise which, unfortunately, we are unable to answer:

1. What is the psychological cause of these rapid and regular variations of the cœnæsthesis? Upon this point only hypotheses are offered (condition of the vascular system, inhibitory action, etc.).

2. What is the principle by which each form of the cœnæsthesis is attached to certain forms of association, to the exclusion of others? We do not know. We can only affirm that in periodic amnesia conservation remains intact; that is to say, that the cellular modifications and dynamic associations subsist; the power of reproduction alone is lost. The associations are provided with two sources of activity: a state (A) is able to stimulate certain groups, but is incapable of influencing others; another state (B) has also certain attached groups; certain elements enter equally into each complexus, and there is incomplete disruption of the memory.

In a word, two psychological states determine by alternation two cœnæstheses, which in turn determine two forms of association and, consequently, two memories.

To complete this portion of our subject, something should be said of the inherent co-operation established, in spite of long interruptions, between states of the same nature, notably in successive attacks of somnambulism. This phenomenon, interesting in many ways, can be examined here only from the point of view of periodical and regular excitations of the same recollections. Curious as this may seem at first glance, it is logical, and perfectly in accord with our conception of the *Ego*. For, if the *Ego* is at any given moment only the sum of actual states of consciousness, and of those vital processes upon which consciousness depends, it is evident that, every time the physiological and psychological complexus is re-formed, the *Ego* will correspond, and similar associations will be brought into action. During each attack a certain physiological state is produced, and, as sensation is for the most part confined to exterior excitation, many associations will not be awakened. There is a simplification of mental life, reduction to an almost mechanical condition. Moreover, it is plain that these states bear a great resemblance to one another, by reason even of their simplicity, and that they differ totally from the normal state. It is natural, then, that the same conditions should produce the same effects, that the same elements should unite in the same combinations, and that the same associations should be awakened to the exclusion of others. They find in the pathological state conditions of existence which are wanting in the normal state, or, at least, are in antagonism with others. In the healthy and normal state, the phenomena of consciousness are too numerous and varied to permit many chances for the same combination to be repeated. It sometimes happens, however, from unknown causes.

A dissenting minister, apparently in good health, went through the entire pulpit service one Sunday morning with perfect consistency—his choice of hymns and lessons and extempore prayer being all related to the subject of the sermon. On the Sunday following he went through the service in precisely the same manner, selecting the same hymns and lessons, offering the same prayer, giving out the same text, and preaching the same sermon. On descending from the pulpit he had not the slightest remembrance of having gone through precisely the same service on the preceding Sunday. He was much alarmed, and feared an attack of brain-disease, but nothing of the kind supervened.* Drunkenness is sometimes marked by a similar return of memory, as in the well known case of the Irish porter who, having lost a package while drunk, got drunk again and remembered where he had left it. As we said at the beginning of this section, cases of periodic amnesia, however curious they may be, teach us much more with regard to the nature of

* Carpenter, *op. cit.*, p. 444.

the *Ego* than to that of memory. But they have their value in mental pathology, and we shall return to them again in the pages which follow.

III.

In progressive amnesia the work of dissolution is slow and continuous, resulting in complete destruction of memory; this is the general rule, but there are exceptions where the morbid evolution does not end in total extinction. The development of the disease is very simple; being gradual in its action, there is little to excite surprise; but it is a fruitful theme for study, since, in learning of the dissolution of memory, we also learn how it is organized. We have no peculiar, rare, or exceptional cases to detail. There is a morbid type, well-nigh constant, which it will suffice to describe.

The primal source of disease is a progressive lesion of the brain (cerebral hemorrhage, apoplexy, softening, general paralysis, atrophy). During the initial period only partial disorders are manifested. The patient is forgetful, and always of the most recent events. A task interrupted is forgotten. Incidents of the day, an order received, or a resolution made—these are soon effaced. Partial amnesia is a common symptom in general paralysis in its earlier stages. Lunatic asylums are full of patients of this class, who, on the day after entry, insist that they have been there for a year, five years, ten years; who have only the vaguest recollection of leaving their homes and their families; and who can tell neither the day of the week nor the name of the month. But recollection of what was done and acquired prior to the disease is retained with great tenacity. Every one has noticed in aged persons that loss of memory is very marked only in respect to the immediate past.

At this point the resources of the old psychology are exhausted. The conclusion, tacit, at least, is that the dissolution of the memory follows no law. We shall endeavor to prove the contrary.

To discover this law it is essential that the progress of dementia should be studied from a psychological point of view.* When the premonitory period just spoken of is passed, there is a gradual and extended decay of all the faculties until the subject is reduced to a vegetative condition. Physicians distinguish between different kinds of dementia according to causes, classing them as senile, paralytic, epileptic, etc. These distinctions have no interest for us. The progress of mental dissolution is at bottom the same, whatever the cause, and that to us is the

* The word *dementia* is here used in a medical sense, and not as a synonym of insanity.

only fact with which we have to concern ourselves. The question now arises, Does loss of memory in this dissolution follow any regular order?

Specialists who have left descriptions of dementia have paid no attention to this question, to them of little importance. Their testimony would be of slight value if we could not derive from it some response; fortunately we are able to apply it in this direction. If we consult the best authorities (Griesinger, Baillarger, Fabret, Foville, and others), we find that amnesia, limited at first to recent events, extends to ideas, then to sentiments and affections, and finally to actions. Here we have the data for the formulation of a law. To classify them, it is enough to examine the different groups.

1. It is a fact of such common experience that the failing memory first loses its hold upon recent events that the anomaly is unobserved. *A priori* it would be natural to believe that the latest impressions were the most distinct and the most stable; and in the normal state this is true. But, with the beginning of dementia, there is grave anatomical lesion, a degeneration of the nervous cells. These elements, a prey to atrophy, are no longer capable of the conservation of new impressions. In precise terms, neither a new modification in the cells, nor the formation of

new dynamical associations, is possible, or, at least, permanent. The anatomical conditions of stability and revivification are wanting. If the perception is entirely new, it is either not registered at all in the nervous centers, or, if registered, the impression is faint and soon effaced.* If it is only a repetition of previous experience still vital, the patient relegates the event to the past; the concomitant circumstances soon vanish, and there are no means for localization in time. But modifications established for years in the nervous elements until they have become organic—dynamical associations and groups of associations called into activity hundreds and thousands of times—these remain; they have a great power of resisting destructive agencies. In this manner we explain a parodox of the memory: the new perishes and the old endures.

2. Soon the primitive bases upon which the patient has been for a time able to live begin in their turn to crumble away. Intellectual acquisitions—the technique of science and art, professional knowledge, the command of foreign languages—disappear little by little. Personal recollections are obliterated, descending toward the past. Those of infancy are the last to disap-

* In a case of senile dementia the patient never recognized his physician, although the latter came to visit him every day for fourteen months.—Felmann, "Archiv. für Psychiatrie," 1864.

pear. Even in an advanced stage of the malady, experiences and songs of childhood often return. Sometimes the subject forgets the greater portion of his own language. Expressions are revived, as it were, by accident; but, ordinarily, any words that may remain in the memory are repeated over and over in a purely automatic way (*vide* Griesinger, Baillarger). The anatomical cause of this intellectual dissolution is an atrophy which, first invading the exterior cerebral layers, penetrates to the white substance, causing a fatty and atheromatous degeneration of the cells, tubes, and capillaries of the nervous tissue.

3. The most careful observers have remarked that the emotional faculties are effaced much more slowly than the intellectual faculties. At first thought it seems strange that states so vague as those pertaining to the feelings should be more stable than ideas and intellectual states in general. Reflection will show that the feelings are the most profound, the most common, and the most tenacious of all phases of mental activity. While knowledge is acquired and objective, feelings are innate. Primarily considered, independently of any subtle or complex forms which they may assume, they are the immediate and permanent expression of organic life. The viscera, the muscles, the bones—all the essential elements of the body—contribute some-

thing to their formation. Feelings form the self; amnesia of the feelings is the destruction of the self. It is logical, then, that a period should arrive when disorganization becomes so great as to disintegrate personality.

4. Those acquisitions which are the last to succumb are almost entirely organic, such as the routine of daily life and habits long contracted. Many are able to arise, dress themselves, take their meals regularly, occupy themselves in manual labor, play at cards or other games—frequently with remarkable skill—while possessing neither judgment, will, nor affections. This automatic activity, which requires only a minimum of conscious memory, belongs to that inferior order of memory having its seat in the cerebral ganglia, the medulla, and the spinal cord.

We thus see that the progressive destruction of memory follows a logical order—a law. *It advances progressively from the unstable to the stable.* It begins with the most recent recollections, which, lightly impressed upon the nervous elements, rarely repeated and consequently having no permanent associations, represent organization in its feeblest form. It ends with the sensorial, instinctive memory, which, become a permanent and integral part of the organism, represents organization in its most highly developed stage. From the first term of the series to the last the movement of amnesia is governed by natural forces, and follows the path of least resistance—that is to say, of least organization. Thus pathology confirms what we have already postulated of the memory, viz., that the process of organization is variable and is comprised between two extreme limits : the new state—organic registration.

This law, which I shall designate as *the law of regression or reversion*, seems to me to be a natural conclusion from the observed facts. However, that all doubts and objections may be removed, it will perhaps be well to subject the law to further test. If memory in the process of decay follows invariably the path just indicated, it should follow the same path in a contrary direction in the process of growth; forms which are the last to disappear should be the first to manifest themselves, since they are the most stable and the synthesis progresses from the lower to the higher.

It is extremely difficult to find cases appropriate to our purpose. The first requirement is that the memory should return of itself. Cases of re-education prove very little. Moreover, progressive amnesia is rarely followed by recovery. Finally, attention having never been called to this point, the records are defective. Physicians occupied with other symptoms usually content themselves with noting that memory "gradually returned."

In the "Essai" previously cited, Louyer-Villermay remarks that when memory is re-established it follows in its return an inverse order to that observed in its dissolution—concrete facts, adjectives, substantives, proper names. There is little to be derived from so confused a statement. In the following we have more definite material to work upon:

"There is a case of a celebrated Russian astronomer who forgot in turn events of recent experience, then those of the year, then those of the latter portion of his life, the breach continually widening until only remembrance of childhood remained. The case was thought to be hopeless. But dissolution suddenly ceased, and repair began; the breach was gradually bridged over in a contrary direction; recollections of youth appeared, then those of middle age, then the experiences of later years, and, finally, the most recent events. His memory was entirely restored at the time of his death." *

The following observation is still more precise; the symptoms were noted from hour to hour. I transcribe it almost entire: †

* Taine, "De l'intelligence," t. i, liv. ii, ch. ii, § 4.

† "Observation sur un cas de perte de mémoire," by M. Kömp-

"I must first give a few details, apparently insignificant of themselves, but worth knowing, since they relate to a remarkable phenomenon. During the latter part of November, an officer of my regiment had his left foot injured by the pressure of an ill-fitting boot. On the 30th of November he went to Versailles to meet his brother. He dined there, returning to Paris the same night, and, on entering his lodgings, found a letter from his father on the mantel-piece. We now come to the important point. On the first of December this officer was at the riding-school, and, his horse falling, he was thrown, striking upon the right side of his body, and particularly upon the right parietal. The shock was followed by a slight syncope. On coming to himself, he remounted 'to drive off a little giddiness,' and continued his lesson for three quarters of an hour with much assiduity. From time to time, however, he kept saying to the riding-master, 'I have been dreaming. What has happened to me?' He was finally taken home. Living in the same house with the patient, I was immediately called in. He was standing, recognized me and greeted me as usual, saying, 'I seem to have been dreaming. What has happened to me?' His speech is natural, he replies readily to all questions,

fen in the "Mémoires de l'Académie de Médecine," 1835, t. iv, p. 489.

and complains only of a confused feeling in the head.

"Notwithstanding my inquiries, and those of the riding-master, and of his servant, he remembers neither the injury to his foot, nor his journey to Versailles, nor going out in the morning, nor the orders he gave on going out, nor his fall, nor what followed. He recognizes every one, calls each visitor by his name, and knows his position as officer. I have not allowed an hour to pass without examining the patient. Each time that I go back he believes that I have come for the first time. He remembers nothing of the prescribed remedies administered (foot-bath, rubbing, etc.). In a word, nothing exists for him except the action of the moment.

"Six hours after the accident—the pulse begins to rise, and the patient takes cognizance of the reply already made so many times, 'You fell from your horse!'

"Eight hours after the accident—the pulse is still rising. The patient remembers to have seen me once before.

"Two hours and a half later—the pulse is normal. The patient no longer forgets what is said to him. He remembers distinctly the injury to his foot. He begins also to recall his visit to Versailles yesterday, but so indistinctly that he says if any one were to affirm positively to the contrary he would be disposed to believe him. However, the memory continuing to return, by night he became firmly convinced that he had been to Versailles. But here the progress of recollection ceased for the day. He went to bed without remembering what he had done at Versailles, how he had returned to Paris, or the receipt of his father's letter.

"December 2d—after a night of tranquil sleep, he remembers on awakening what he did at Versailles, how he came back, and that he found a letter from his father on the mantel-piece. But of all that he saw or heard on the 1st of December, before his fall, he is still ignorant to-day—that is to say, he has no knowledge of the events in question save from the testimony of others.

"This loss of memory is, as the mathematicians say, inversely as the time that has elapsed between any given incident and the fall, and the return of memory is in a determinate order from the most distant to the most near."

Is not this observation, made at random by a man who is apparently greatly surprised at what he records, a satisfactory proof? It is true that it was only a question of temporary and limited amnesia; but we see that even within these narrow limits the law is verified. I regret my inability to place before the reader more facts of this kind, notwithstanding an extended search.

When attention is called to this point, I hope that other material will be discovered. On the whole, our law, derived from facts and verified by observation, may be assumed as true until the contrary is proved. It may be further corroborated by other known facts.

This law, general when applied to memory, is only one phase of a still more general law in biology. It is a well-known fact in organic life that structures last formed are the first to degenerate. It is, says a physiologist, analogous to what occurs in a great commercial crisis. The old houses resist the storm; the new houses, less solid, go down on every side. Finally, in the biological world, dissolution acts in a contrary direction to evolution: it proceeds from the complex to the simple. Hughlings Jackson was the first to show that the higher functions—the complex, special, voluntary functions of the nervous system—were the first to disappear; that the lower, the simple, general automatic functions were the last to go. We have stated these two facts in the dissolution of memory: the new perishes before the old, the complex before the simple. The law which we have formulated is only the psychological expression of a law of life, and pathology shows in its turn that memory is a biological fact. The study of periodic amnesia has thrown much light upon our subject. In showing us how the memory is dissolved and reconstructed, it teaches us what memory is. It has revealed a law which permits us to observe morbid types in great variety and from many points of view; later on, we shall, by its aid, be able to include them in one general survey.

Without attempting a careful review in this place, let us recall briefly what has been observed above. First, in all cases, abolition of recent impressions; in periodic amnesia, total suspension of all forms of memory, except those which are semi-organized and organic; in total and temporary amnesia, complete loss of memory, except in its organic forms; in one instance (Macnish) amnesia comprising even organic forms. We shall see in the following chapter that partial disorders of memory are governed by this same law of regression, and especially the most important group—that of amnesia of language.

The law of regression being admitted, we have now to determine in what manner it acts. Upon this point I shall be brief, having only hypotheses to offer. It would be puerile to suppose that recollections are arranged in the brain in the form of layers in order of age, after the fashion of geological strata, and that disease, penetrating from the surface to the lowest point, acts like an experimentalist removing the brain of an animal, bit by bit. To explain the action of the morbid process we must have recourse to the hypothesis advanced above with regard to the physical bases of memory. It may be summed up in a few words.

It is very probable that recollections occupy the same anatomical seat as primitive impressions, and that they excite the activity of the same nervous elements (cells and filaments). The latter may have very different positions from the surface of the brain to the spinal cord. Conservation and reproduction depend: (1) upon a certain modification of the cells; (2) upon the formation of more or less complex groups which we have designated as dynamic associations. Such are the physical bases of memory.

Primitive acquisitions, those that date from infancy, are the most simple; they include the formation of secondary automatic movements in the education of the senses. They depend principally upon the medulla and the lower centers of the brain; and we know that at this period of life the exterior cerebral layers are imperfectly developed. Aside from their simplicity there is every reason why these first acquisitions should be stable. In the first place, the impressions are received in virgin elements. Nutrition is very active; but incessant molecular repair serves only to fix the registered perception; the new molecules taking the exact places occupied by the old, the acquired state finally becomes organic. Moreover, the dynamic associations formed between the different elements attain after a time to a condition of complete fusion, thanks to continual repetition. It is inevitable, then, that the earlier acquisitions should be better conserved and more easily reproduced than any others, and that they should constitute the most lasting form of memory.

While the adult organism is in a healthy state, new impressions and associations, although of a much more complex order than those of infancy, have still great chances of stability. The causes just enumerated are always in action, although with modified energy. But if, through the effects of old age or disease, the conditions change; if the vital processes, particularly nutrition, begin to fail; if waste is in excess of repair—then the impressions become unstable and the associations weak. Take an example. A man is at that period of progressive amnesia when forgetfulness of recent impressions is very rapid. He attends a recital, looks at a landscape, or witnesses a play. The psychical experience consists primarily of a sum of auditory or optical impressions forming certain very complex groups. In the registered perceptions of this particular recital or this particular play there is, generally speaking, nothing new except in the grouping, the associations. Sounds, forms, and colors, forming the substance of the event, have long been matters of experience, and have been many times memorized. But, because of the morbid condition of the brain, this new complexus can not be fixed; the component elements enter into other associations, groups of greater stability formed in a healthy state and often revived. Between the new complexus, tending feebly to assert itself, and the old associations, strongly established, the struggle is very unequal. It is more than probable, therefore, that the primitive combinations would be revived later on, even in place of the new. These explanations will suffice. It should be noted, however, that the hypothesis with regard to the cause of progressive amnesia is of secondary importance. Whether it is accepted or rejected, the value of our law is unchanged.

IV.

There is little to be said upon the subject of congenital amnesia. It is considered here that our discussion may be complete. Cases are met with in idiots, imbeciles, and, to a minor degree, in cretins. Most of these are afflicted with a general debility of memory. Varying with the subject, amnesia may extend so far in some instances as to prevent the acquisition and conservation of the ordinary acts that go to make up the routine of life. But, while weakness of the memory is the rule, frequent exceptions are found. Among victims of congenital amnesia there are some whose memories, within certain limits, have been very remarkable.

It has long been observed that in many idiots and imbeciles the senses are very unequally developed; thus, the hearing may be of extreme delicacy and precision, while the other senses are blunted. The arrest of development is not uniform in all respects. It is not surprising, then, that general weakness of memory should co-exist in the same subject with the evolution and even hypertrophy of a particular memory. Thus, certain idiots, insensible to all other impressions, have an extraordinary taste for music, and are able to retain an air which they have once heard. In rare instances there is a memory for forms and colors, and an aptitude for drawing. Cases of memory of figures, dates, proper names, and words in general, are more common. An idiot "could remember the day when every person had been buried in the parish for thirty-five years, and could repeat with unvarying accuracy the name and age of the deceased, and the mourners at the funeral. Out of the line of burials he had not one idea, could not give an intelligible reply to a single question, nor be trusted even to feed himself."* Certain idiots, unable to make the most elementary arithmetical calculations, repeat the whole of the multiplication table without an error. Others recite, word for word, passages that have been read to them, and can not learn the letters of the alphabet. Drobisch reports the following case of which he was an observer: A boy of fourteen, almost an idiot, experienced great trouble in learning to read. He had, nevertheless, a marvelous facility for remembering the order in which words and letters succeeded one another. When allowed two or three minutes in which to glance over the page of a book printed in a language which he did not know, or treating of subjects of which he was ignorant, he could, in the brief time mentioned, repeat every word from memory exactly as if the book remained open before him.† The existence of this partial memory is so common that it has been utilized in the education of idiots and imbeciles.‡ It is worth noting that

* Forbes Winslow, *op. cit.*, p. 561.

† Drobisch, "Empirische Psychologie," p. 95.—Dr. Herzen has told me of the case of a Russian, aged twenty-seven, who became an imbecile through excessive dissipation. He retained nothing of the brilliant talents of his youth with the exception of an extraordinary memory, being able to work out at sight the most difficult problems in arithmetic and algebra, and to repeat, word for word, long passages of poetry after a single reading.

‡ See, on this subject, Ireland "On Idiocy and Imbecility," London, 1877.

idiots attacked by mania or some other acute disease frequently display a temporary memory. Thus, "an idiot, in a fit of anger, told of a complicated incident of which he had been a witness long before, and which at the time seemed to have made no impression upon him." *

In cases of congenital amnesia, the exceptions are the most instructive. The law only confirms a common truth—viz., that memory depends upon the constitution of the brain, and that in idiots and imbeciles the condition is abnormal. But the formation of limited partial memories will aid us in the comprehension of certain disorders to which we have not yet referred. I am inclined to believe that a careful study of mental symptoms in idiots would permit us to determine the anatomical and physiological conditions of memory. To this point we shall return in the following chapter.

* Griesinger, *op. cit.*, p. 431.

CHAPTER III.

PARTIAL AMNESIA.

I.

BEFORE taking up the subject of partial amnesia, something remains to be said with regard to the varieties of memory. Without preliminary explanation, the facts which we shall cite would appear inexplicable and almost miraculous. That a person should be deprived of all recollection of words and retain the other faculties intact; that he should forget one language and retain his mastery of others; that a language long forgotten should suddenly return; that there should be loss of memory for music and for nothing else—these are facts so singular at first thought that, if they were not recorded by the most trustworthy observers, we would be inclined to class them with popular fables. If, on the contrary, we once have an accurate idea of what the word memory really means, the marvelous element disappears, and these facts, far from exciting our wonder, are seen to be the natural and logical consequences of a morbid influence.

The use of the word memory in a general sense is perfectly justifiable. It designates a faculty common to all sentient and thinking beings—the possibility of conserving and reproducing impressions. But the history of psychology shows that it is too often forgotten that this general term, like all others of its class, is of value only when applied to particular cases, and that *memory* may be resolved into *memories*, just as the life of an organism may be resolved into the lives of the organs, the tissues, the anatomical elements, which compose it. "The ancient and still unexploded error," says Lewes, "which treats memory as an independent function, a faculty, for which a separate organ, or seat, is sought, arises from the tendency continually to be noticed of personifying an abstraction. Instead of recognizing it as the short-hand expression for what is common to all concrete facts of remembrance, or for the sum of such facts, many writers suppose it to have an existence apart." *

While common experience has long demonstrated the natural inequality of different forms of memory in the same individual, psychologists have either neglected this point or have denied its truthfulness. Dugald Stewart seriously affirms

* *Op. cit.*, prob. ii, p. 119.

that "original disparities among men in this respect are by no means so immense as they seem to be at first view, and that much is to be ascribed to different habits of attention, and to a difference of selection among the various objects and events presented to their curiosity." * Gall, the first to protest against this view, assigned to each faculty its own special memory, and denied the existence of memory as an independent function.†

Contemporary psychology, more comprehensive and exact in its investigations, has discovered a considerable number of facts which leave no doubt with regard to the inequality of memories in the same person. Think, for instance, of artists like Horace Vernet and Gustave Doré painting a portrait from memory; of chess players able to carry on one or several games in the mind; of lightning calculators like Zerah Colburn, who "see the figures before their eyes"; ‡ of the man spoken of by Lewes, who, after walking half a mile through a crowded street, was able to name all the shops he had passed in relative order; of Mozart, writing down the "Miserere" in the Sistine Chapel after having heard it twice. For

* "Philosophy of the Human Mind," p. 307.

† "Fonctions du cerveau," t. i.

‡ I have had occasion to note that several calculators do not see the figures in their problems, but *hear* them. It matters little, so far as our theory is concerned, whether the images are visual or auditory.

further details the reader is referred to special contributions on this subject.* The question can not be considered in detail here. It will suffice for my purpose if these inequalities of memory are granted.

What are we to infer from these partial memories? The special development of a certain sense with the anatomical structures upon which it depends. Let us take a particular case, a good visual memory, for instance. Its conditions are that the eye, the optic nerve, and those portions of the brain concurring in the act of vision (that is—according to generally received opinion in anatomy—certain portions of the pons Varolii, the crura cerebri, the optic tract, and the cerebral hemispheres) should be finely developed and act harmoniously. These structures, superior by hypothesis to the average, are perfectly adapted to receive and transmit impressions. Consequently, the modifications of the nervous elements, as well as the dynamical associations which are formed (and these, as we have several times pointed out, are the bases of memory), ought to be more stable, more definite, and easier to revive than those formed in a less favored brain. In short, when we say that the visual organ has a good anatomical and physiological constitution, we

* Lewes, *op. cit.;* Luys, "Le cerveau et ses fonctions," p. 120; Taine, *op. cit.*, t. i, 1[re] partie, liv. ii, ch. i.

state the conditions of a good visual memory. We may go further, and note that the phrase "a good visual memory" is still too indefinite. Does not daily observation show us that some persons remember forms most easily, while others have a special facility for recalling colors? It is reasonable to suppose that the first memory depends upon the muscular sensibility of the eye, the second upon the retina and the nervous apparatus connected therewith. These remarks are applicable to hearing, smell, taste, and those diverse forms of sensibility comprised under the general term touch—in fact, to all the sense-perceptions. If we think of the intimate relations existing between the feelings, the emotions, the general sensibility and physical constitution of each person, if we remember how much these physical states depend upon the organs of animal life, we are able to understand that they bear the same relations to the feelings as do the organs of sense to the perceptions. According to constitutional differences, transmitted impressions may be weak or intense, stable or fleeting; so it is with the conditions modifying the memory of feelings. The preponderance of any system of organs over another gives superiority to the corresponding group of recollections. There remain the psychical states of a higher order, abstract ideas and complex sentiments. These can not be referred directly to any particular organ or organs; the seat of their production and reproduction is not yet localized with anything like precision. But, as they manifestly result from the association or disassociation of primitive states, we have no reason to suppose that they are governed by any other principle than that already designated.

In the same person, then, an unequal development of the different senses and different organs induces unequal modifications in the corresponding portions of the nervous system; hence unequal conditions of recollection, and, finally, varieties of memory. It is even probable that inequality of memories in the same person is the rule rather than the exception. As we have no exact process by which we can analyze each case separately and compare it with others, what we have said above is conjectural, although we insist that it applies to all cases of inequality where great disproportion is shown. The antagonism existing between different forms of memory might further provide us with indirect proof of our hypothesis; it is a field in which important discoveries are yet to be made; but it lies outside the province of this work.* Finally, the influence of education must not be forgotten. Its *rôle* is evidently an important one; but education applies in the main only

* See Spencer's "Principles of Psychology," p. 228, *et seq.*

to faculties previously set in relief by nature; and in many cases it is unable to extend its sphere of action to other and less favored mental traits. In psychology, as in every other domain of practical science, experience alone is the final arbitrator. We may observe, however, that the relative independence of different forms of memory may be established by reason alone. It is, in fact, a corollary to the two general propositions which follow:

1. Every recollection has its seat in a definite and determinate portion of the encephalon;

2. The encephalon and the cerebral hemispheres are made up of a certain number of totally differentiated organs, each having its special function to perform, while remaining in the most intimate relations with its fellows.

This last proposition is now admitted by most authorities upon the nervous system. But I do not wish to dwell upon this point.

In physiology the distinction of partial memories is a familiar truth; * but in psychology the method of "faculties" has so long forced the recognition of memory as an entity that the exist-

* See in particular Ferrier, "Functions of the Brain." Gratiolet ("Anat. comparée," t. ii, p. 460) says that each sense has a corresponding and correlative memory, and that the mind, like the body, has its temperaments which result from the preponderance of a given order of sensations in manifestations of mental activity.

ence of partial memories has been wholly ignored, or, at the most, regarded as anomalous. It is time that this misconception was done away with, and that the fact of special, or, as some authors prefer, *local* memories, was clearly recognized. This last term we accept willingly on the condition that it is interpreted as a disseminated localization, according to the theory of dynamic associations advanced above. The memory has often been compared to a store-house where every fact is preserved in its proper place. If this metaphor is to be retained, it must be presented in a more active form; we may compare each particular memory, for instance, with a contingent of clerks charged with a special and exclusive service. Any one of these departments might be abolished without serious detriment to the rest of the work; and that is what happens in partial disorders of the memory.

We come now to the pathology of our subject. If, in the normal condition of the organism, the different forms of memory are relatively independent, it is natural that, if in a morbid state one disappears, the others should remain intact. The process needs no explanation, since it results from the very nature of memory. It is true that many partial disorders are not restricted to a single group of recollections. This is not surprising when we remember the close association which exists between the different parts of the brain, their functions, and their corresponding psychical states. There are cases, however, in which amnesia is very limited.

A complete study of partial amnesia would necessitate the consideration, one after another, of the different manifestations of psychical activity, with the purpose of demonstrating that each group of recollections may be in turn suppressed, temporarily or permanently. Such a task, however, is impossible of fulfillment. We can not even say that certain forms are never partly effaced, and that they disappear only with the complete dissolution of the memory. We must be content to await the more extended and definite pathological contributions which the future may bring forth.

Strictly speaking, there is only one form of partial amnesia concerning which existing knowledge will warrant a complete analysis—that of signs (spoken or written, interjections, gestures). The facts collected are abundant and are explicable by the law formulated above. Reserving cases of this kind for separate study, we shall first review what is known of other forms of partial amnesia.

Persons, according to Calmeil,* have lost the

* "Dictionnaire," en trente volumes, article "Amnésie."

power of reproducing certain tones or colors, and have been forced to give up music or painting. Others lose only the memory of numbers, forms, a foreign language, proper names, the existence of their nearest relatives. The case recorded by Sir H. Holland has been often cited.

"I descended on the same day," he says, "two very deep mines in the Hartz Mountains, remaining some hours underground in each. While in the second mine, and exhausted both from fatigue and inanition, I felt the utter impossibility of talking longer with the German inspector who accompanied me. Every German word and phrase deserted my recollection; and it was not until I had taken food and wine, and been some time at rest, that I regained them again."* This case, although the best known of its class, is not unique. Dr. Beattie relates that one of his friends, having received a blow on the head, lost all his knowledge of Greek, although his memory was otherwise unimpaired. The loss of languages acquired by study has often been observed as a result of certain acute febrile diseases. The same thing is noticed with regard to music. A child, having received a severe blow on the head, remained for three days unconscious. On coming to himself, he was found to have forgotten

* "Chapters on Mental Physiology," p. 160.

all that he had learned of music. Nothing else was lost.*

There are more complicated cases. A patient, who had completely forgotten the value of musical notes, was able to play an air after hearing it. Another was able to write down notes, and even to compose, recognizing the melody by the sense of hearing; but he could not play with the notes before him.† These facts, showing the complexity of what are apparently the simplest of the mental functions, will be considered further on.‡ Sometimes the most perfectly organized and the most stable recollections disappear momentarily, while others of the same nature remain intact. A surgeon, who was thrown from his horse and remained for some time insensible, described the accident distinctly upon his recovery, and gave minute directions with regard to his own treatment. But he lost all idea of having either wife or children, and this condition lasted for three days.# Is this case to be explained by mental automatism? The subject, while partly unconscious, retained all his professional knowledge. Certain patients lose entirely the memory of proper names, even of their own.

* Carpenter, "Mental Physiology," p. 441.

† Kussmaul, "Die Störungen der Sprache," p. 181; Proust, "Archives générales de médecine," 1872.

‡ See § II, following.

Abercrombie, "Essay on the Intellectual Powers," p. 156.

We shall see hereafter, in studying the amnesia of signs throughout its complete evolution—as shown particularly in the aged—that proper names are always forgotten first. In the following cases, this forgetfulness was a symptom of softening of the brain.

A man, being unable to recollect the name of a friend, drags his companion through several streets to the house of the gentleman of whom he was speaking, and points to the name-plate on the door.

Mr. Von B., formerly envoy to Madrid, and afterward to St. Petersburg, was about to make a visit, but could not tell the servants his name. "Turning round immediately to a gentleman who accompanied him, he said, with much earnestness, 'For God's sake, tell me who I am!' The question excited laughter, but, as Mr. Von B. insisted on being answered, adding that he had entirely forgotten his own name, he was told it, upon which he finished his visit." *

In others the apoplectic attack is followed only by amnesia of numbers. A traveler, exposed for a long period to the cold, experienced great weakness of memory. He could neither perform any mathematical calculation, nor could he retain for a moment the result of any such calculation made by another. Forgetfulness of

* Forbes Winslow, *op. cit.*, pp. 265–269.

persons is of very frequent occurrence, a fact not at all surprising, since this form of memory, even in its normal state, is very slightly developed and unstable in many individuals, resulting as it does from a complex mental synthesis. A striking example is given by Louyer-Villermay. "An old man in the company of his wife believed himself all the while with another woman whom he had been accustomed to visit frequently, and exclaimed, continually, 'Madame, I can remain no longer; I must go back to my wife and children.'" * Carpenter tells us of a gentleman of considerable scientific ability with whom he had been intimate from childhood, that, after passing his seventieth year, although unusually vigorous in body, he was forgetful of circumstances which had happened not long previously, and occasionally was unable to comprehend unusual words. "Though continually at the British Museum, the Royal Society, and the Geological Society, he would be unable to refer to either by name, but would speak of 'that public place.' He still continued his visits to his friends, and recognized them in their own homes, or in other places (as the Scientific Societies) where he had been accustomed to meet them; but the writer, on meeting him at the house of

* Louyer-Villermay, "Dictionnaire de science et médecine," article "Mémoire."

one of the oldest friends of both, usually residing in London, but then staying at Brighton, found that he was not recognized; and the same want of recognition showed itself when the meeting took place out of doors. The want of memory of words then showed itself more conspicuously; one word being substituted for another, sometimes in a manner that showed the chain of association to be (as it were) bent or distorted. . . . Thus . . . he told a friend that 'he had had his umbrella washed,' the meaning of which was gradually discovered to be that he had had his hair cut."* His health continued good for some time, but his memory progressively failed. He finally died of apoplexy.

In this instance there was at the same time amnesia of proper names and amnesia of persons, but the most curious fact in connection with such cases is the operation of the law of contiguity. Recognition of persons does not come of itself through the simple fact of their presence. It must be suggested, or rather aided, by actual impression of the circumstances in which they are commonly presented. Recollection of places, fixed by life-long experience, becomes almost organic and remains stable. It serves as a *point d'appui* for the excitation of other remembrances. The name of the place may not be revived; asso-

* *Op. cit.*, p. 545.

ciation between the object and sign is often too weak. But recollection of the person follows, since it depends upon a very stable form of association—contiguity in space. The surviving category of recollections aids in the revival of others, which, left to themselves, would have remained inactive. A more extended enumeration of cases of partial amnesia would be easy, but without profit to the reader. It is enough to know their general nature from occasional illustration.

The question naturally arises, whether forms of memory totally or temporarily disorganized by disease are those most perfectly established, or those, on the contrary, which are the feeblest. To this we have no positive answer. Reason alone teaches us that morbid influences follow the path of least resistance. Observation seems to confirm that hypothesis. In most cases of partial amnesia the least stable forms of memory are effaced. I do not know of a single case where, any organic form having been suspended or abolished, the higher forms remained intact. It would be hazardous to affirm, however, that this rule is invariable. To the question propounded we can, therefore, reply only by hypothesis in the present state of knowledge. Moreover, it would be contrary to the scientific method to apply a general law off-hand to a series of heterogeneous cases, each depending upon special conditions.

A careful analysis of each case, and of its causes, is necessary before it would be possible to assert that all are reducible to a single formula. But the present state of our knowledge will not permit of such extended study.

The same remarks are applicable to the method by which amnesia is produced. We know nothing of the physiological conditions relating to each form. As to psychological conditions, we must fall back on hypothesis. Cases of partial amnesia may be divided into two classes—those of destruction, and those of suspension of the mental functions. The first are direct results of disorganization of the nervous elements. In the second, certain groups are temporarily isolated and impotent; in psychological terms, they are without the mechanism of association. The case cited by Carpenter, last quoted, suggests some such explanation. The close solidarity existing between the different portions of the encephalon, and, consequently, between the different psychical states, generally speaking, persists. Certain groups alone, with the sum of recollections which they represent, are in some degree rendered inactive, and, cut off from the influence of other groups, are for a time unable to enter into consciousness. This state results from physiological conditions of which we are ignorant.

II.

One form of partial amnesia, that of *signs*, we have reserved for special study. The term we here use in its widest meaning as comprising all methods adopted by man to express his sentiments and ideas. The subject is almost unlimited, and is rich in facts at once similar to and different from one another, since they have a common psychological character and yet differ in nature as to whether they are vocal or written, or are to be classed as gestures, or come under the head of drawing or music. They are easily observed, accurately localized, and, through their variety, lend themselves readily to comparative analysis. We shall see, moreover, that cases of partial amnesia belonging in this category verify in a remarkable manner the law of the dissolution of memory outlined in the preceding chapter.

To prevent misconception, we may say here that we do not propose a detailed study of aphasia. It is true that in most cases aphasia is connected with a disordered memory, but there are other influences to be considered which do not concern us. The investigations made during the last forty years with regard to diseases of language show that the term aphasia is very general in its application. Aphasia, being not a disease but a symptom, varies with the morbid and inducing cause. Thus certain victims of aphasia are deprived of every mode of expression; others are able to speak but can not write, or *vice versa;* aphasia of gesture is very rare. Sometimes the patient retains an extensive vocabulary of vocal and graphic signs, but can not use it correctly (cases of heterophasia and agraphia). Sometimes he does not understand the meaning of words, written or spoken, although the senses of hearing and sight are intact (cases of verbal surdity and cecity). Aphasia is sometimes permanent, sometimes transitory. It is often accompanied by hemiplegia, which is usually right-sided, and, independently of amnesia, is of itself an obstacle to writing.* As there is also variation with the individual, the intricacy of the theme is evident. Happily, it does not lie within the province of this treatise. Our task, already sufficiently difficult, is to separate from disorders of language and those of the expressive faculty in general the cases which seem to pertain to memory alone.

It is clear, in the first place, that we are not concerned with cases of aphasia resulting from idiocy, dementia, or general loss of memory, nor with cases where the faculty of transmission alone is wanting, as in lesion of the white substance in the third left frontal convolution, re-

* Left-handed persons always have hemiplegia on the left side.

sulting in the destruction of the expressive faculty, the gray substance remaining intact.* But this double elimination does not decrease the difficulty, since the majority of cases of aphasia are produced under entirely different conditions. Let us examine the most common type.

I do not think it necessary to cite examples which are easily found. † Aphasia usually comes on very suddenly. The patient is not able to speak, and, on attempting to write, finds himself powerless; at most he can only trace with prolonged effort a few unintelligible words. His countenance shows that he is conscious. He tries to make himself understood by gestures. There is no paralysis of the muscles employed in articulation; the tongue moves freely. Such are the chief characteristics of the attack so far as it is connected with our special object. What has taken place in the psychical state of the patient? is the memory gone? Reflection will show that amnesia of signs is not comparable to

* For cases of this kind see Kussmaul, "Die Störungen der Sprache," p. 99.

† The literature of aphasia is so voluminous that the mere enumeration of titles would fill many pages of this work. From a psychological point of view the reader should consult especially Trousseau, "Clinique médicale," t. ii; Falret, article "Aphasie," in the "Dictionnaire encycl. des sciences médic."; Proust, "Archives générales de médecine," 1872; Kussmaul, "Die Störungen der Sprache" (an important work); Hughlings Jackson, "On the Affections of Speech" in "Brain" for 1878, 1879, 1880.

that of colors, sounds, a foreign language, or a period of life. It includes the whole activity of the mind; in this sense it is general; and yet it is partial, since the patient retains his ideas and recollections, and is conscious of his condition. If we adopt the theory that amnesia of signs is a disease of the motor memory, we discover at once its distinguishing characteristic, and are able to study the subject from a new point of view. The term motor memory is not easily defined in a few words; the subject has received little attention from psychologists, and it is impossible to enlarge upon it here. I have endeavored elsewhere,* although in a tentative and summary way, to explain the psychological importance of movements, and to show that every conscious state depends, to a certain extent, upon the motor elements. Keeping to that portion of the subject with which we are alone concerned, I shall only note, what every one will readily admit, that feelings, ideas, and intellectual actions in general, are not fixed, and only become a portion of memory when there are corresponding residua in the nervous system—residua consisting, as we have previously demonstrated, of nervous elements, and dynamic associations among those elements. On this condition, and this only, can

* "Revue philosophique," October, 1879. See also Maudsley, "Physiology and Pathology of the Mind," part i, chap. viii.

there be conservation and reproduction. But the same must hold true of movements. Those with which we are concerned here, and which are employed in articulate speech, writing, drawing, music, gestures, can only be conserved and reproduced on the condition that there are motor residua constituted as explained above. It is clear that, if nothing remained of a word uttered or written for the first time, it would be impossible to learn to speak or write.

The existence of motor residua being admitted, we are able to understand the nature of amnesia of signs. Intellectual activity consists, as we have said, of a series of conscious states associated in a certain way. Each term in the series appears to the consciousness as a simple fact; but in reality it is not so. When we speak or think with any degree of precision, all the terms in the series form into pairs, each pair composed of the idea and its expression. In the normal state the fusion between the two elements is so complete that they are one; but disease proves that they may be disassociated. Moreover, the expression pair is not sufficiently comprehensive. It is exact only when applied to that portion of the human race which is unable to write. If I think of a house, aside from the mental representation which is the conscious state properly so-called, aside from the vocal sign which translates the idea and is apparently one with it, there is a graphic image almost as closely blended with the idea which in the act of writing predominates over the others. Nor is this all. Around the vocal sign *house* are grouped, by less intimate association, the vocal signs of other languages (*domus*, *maison*, *Haus*, *casa*, etc.). About the graphic sign *house* are grouped the graphic signs of the same languages. We see, then, that in the adult mind every definite state of consciousness is not a simple unity, but a complex unity—a group. The mental representation, the thought, is, properly speaking, only the nucleus; around it are grouped a greater or less number of determining signs. When this is understood, the mechanism of amnesia of signs becomes clear. It is a pathological state in which, the idea remaining intact or very nearly so, a portion or all of the interpreting signs are temporarily or entirely forgotten. This general proposition may be profitably completed with a more detailed study.

1. Is it true that in cases of aphasia the idea subsists while its verbal and graphic expressions have disappeared?

The question is not whether we are able to think without the use of signs. The subject of aphasia has long made use of signs; but does the idea disappear with the possibility of expression?

Facts point to the negative. Although it is generally recognized that aphasia, when serious and of long duration, is always accompanied by mental weakness, there can be no doubt that mental activity persists, even when there are no means of translating the ideas into words or gestures. Examples are numerous; I shall cite only a few of the most important.

Patients deprived of only a part of their vocabulary, but unable to find the proper word, replace it by a paraphrase or description. For scissors they say "the things that cut"; for window, "what you see through." They designate a man by the place where he lives, by his titles, his profession, inventions which he has made, or books that he has written.* In the most serious cases we sometimes find the patient able to play at cards with calculation and discretion; others are able to superintend their affairs. In the latter class was the great landed proprietor spoken of by Trousseau, "who had leases and deeds brought to him, and indicated by gestures, intelligible to his attendants, what changes were to be made, and these were generally reasonable and profitable." A man entirely deprived of speech sent his physi-

* The victim of aphasia often confounds words, says "fire" for "bread," etc., or devises new and unintelligible expressions; but disorders of this kind are more diseases of language than of memory.

cian a detailed history of his case clearly expressed and in a legible hand. We also have the testimony of patients themselves after recovery. "I had forgotten all the words I knew," said one of them, "but I retained fully my consciousness and will-power. I knew very well what I wanted to say, yet could not say it. When you [the physician] questioned me, I understood perfectly; I made every effort to reply, but it was impossible to remember a word."*

Rostran, a physician, suddenly attacked, was unable to speak or write a single word, but "analyzed the symptoms of his malady and sought to connect it with some special lesion of the brain, as if he were in attendance at a medical consultation." In another case, that of Lordat, the patient "was capable of comprehending a lecture and of classifying its heads in his mind, but, when his thoughts sought expression in speech or writing, he was helpless, although there was no paralysis."†

2. Does this amnesia depend, as suggested above, especially upon the motor elements? In establishing the necessary existence of motor

* Legroux, "De l'aphasie," p. 96.

† For details, see Trousseau, *op. cit.* Lordat was an ardent spiritualist, and from that point of view drew conclusions with regard to the independence of the mind. He deceived himself. In the judgment of those who knew him, he did not regain his original faculties after nominal recovery. See Proust, *op. cit.*

residua, this problem was not examined in all its complex relations. We shall therefore return to it again.

When we learn to speak our own tongue or a foreign language, there are certain sounds or acoustic signs which are registered in the brain. But that is only a portion of the task. They must be repeated until they pass from a receptive to an active state, and we are able to translate the acoustic signs into vocal movements. This operation is at first very difficult, since it consists in the co-ordination of very complex movements. We are only able to speak with facility when these movements are easily reproduced—that is to say, when the motor residua are organized. When we learn to write we fix the eyes upon a copy; the visual signs are registered in the brain, and then, with great effort, we endeavor to reproduce them by movement of the hand. Here there is a co-ordination of very delicate movements. We are able to write only when the visual signs are translated immediately into movements—that is to say, when the motor residua are organized. The same remarks are applicable to music, design, or expression by gesture, as in the case of deaf-mutes. The faculty of expression is more complex than it appears to be on general observation. Ideas or sentiments to be expressed require an acoustic (or visual) memory and a motor memory. Why may we not believe that it is the motor memory which is affected in amnesia of signs?

In most cases of aphasia, if a common object, a knife, for instance, is held before the patient and designated by a wrong name, such as "fork" or "book," the patient indicates dissent. Utter the proper word, and there is a gesture of affirmation. If you ask the patient to repeat, he is not usually able to do so. Thus the idea is not only preserved, but also the acoustic sign, since there is a discrimination among many and selection of the one proper to the object. As speech is impossible while the vocal organs remain intact, it must be that amnesia affects the motor elements. A similar experiment may be made in writing; in cases where the victim of aphasia is not paralyzed we arrive at the same results and the same conclusion. The patient has retained the memory of visual signs, while he has lost the memory of movements necessary to their reproduction. Some are able to copy, but when the original is taken away they are helpless.

However, in advancing the theory of motor amnesia as applicable to the majority of cases, I do not pretend that the law is invariable. In so involved a question one should guard against absolute affirmation. In cases of chronic aphasia the patient often forgets vocal and written signs, or at least recognizes them only after great effort and prolonged hesitation. In such cases amnesia is not limited to the motor elements alone. On the other hand, we have seen that in certain cases the patient is able to repeat or copy words. Others can read aloud without being capable of extempore speech; but this is exceptional.* Many, however, are able to read mentally while they can not read aloud. It sometimes happens —although rarely—that the patient is able to utter a portion of a phrase off-hand without being able to begin again. Brown-Séquard records the case of a physician who talked in his sleep, although when awake he was the victim of aphasia. These instances, infrequent as they are, show that motor amnesia is not invariable. It is the same with this as with other forms of memory: under certain exceptional conditions it revives.

An analogy may be cited in passing. The subject of aphasia, in attempting to repeat a word, resembles exactly a person who is only able to recall a fact with the assistance of another: the psychological mechanism of forgetfulness of signs is the same as that of all forgetfulness. It consists of a disassociation. An impression is forgotten when it can not be revived by association, when it does not enter into any series. In aphasia the idea is

* Falret, *op. cit.*, p. 618.

unable to resuscitate its corresponding sign or motor expression. Here the disassociation is more complete. It affects not only the *terms* united by previous experience, but also *elements* which have been so closely welded to one another as to appear to the consciousness as an entity, to sustain whose relative independence would seem the refinement of analytical subtilty, if the disease did not itself afford demonstration.*

It is this close association of the idea, the sign (vocal or written), and the motor element, which renders it so difficult to establish in a definite and indisputable manner that amnesia of signs is, above all, a motor amnesia. As every conscious state tends to translate itself into movement, as, according to Bain, thought is only restrained expression, it is not possible by analysis alone to show definite separation among these three elements. It seems to me, however, that the memory of vocal and written signs which survives in the intelligent subject of aphasia represents what

* Cases long confounded under the general term aphasia have been carefully described of late under the head of *verbal cecity* and *verbal surdity* (*Wortblindheit*, *Worttaubheit*). The patient is able to speak and write; sight and hearing are conserved, and yet the words that he reads or hears pronounced convey no meaning to the mind; to him they are simple optical or acoustic phenomena; they suggest no ideas, and have ceased to be signs. This is another and rarer form of disassociation. For details see Kussmaul, *op. cit.*, ch. xxvii.

is called the "inner voice," that minimum of determination without which the mind would be on the way to dementia, and, consequently, that the motor elements alone are effaced in such instances. On examining the opinions of the few physicians who have made a special study of the psychology of aphasia, I find that their theory does not differ sensibly from my own except in form. "I have asked myself," said Trousseau, "if aphasia is not simply forgetfulness of those instinctive and harmonious movements learned from early infancy and constituting articulate language; and if, by this forgetfulness, the subject of aphasia is not in the condition of a child taught to stammer forth his first words, or of a deaf-mute who, suddenly cured of his deafness, attempts to imitate the speech of persons which he hears for the first time. The difference between the victim of aphasia and the deaf-mute would then be, that one had forgotten what he had learned, and that the other had not yet been taught." *

Kussmaul says: "If we consider memory as a general function of the nervous system, there must be for the combination of sounds into words at once an acoustic memory and a motor memory. Memory of words is thus double: 1, there is a memory for words as far as they may be regarded

* *Op. cit.*, p. 718.

as groups of acoustic phenomena; 2, there is another memory for words as motor images (*Bewegungsbilder*). Trousseau has observed that aphasia may always be reduced to a loss of memory either of vocal signs or of the means by which words are articulated. W. Ogle also distinguishes two verbal memories, the first familiar to every one, through which we have consciousness of a word, and the second through which we are able to express it."*

Is it necessary to admit that the residua corresponding to an idea, those which correspond to its vocal sign, its graphic sign, and to the movements that express the one or the other—must we believe that these are associated in the cortex? What anatomical conclusions are we to draw from the fact that there may be loss of memory of movements without that of innate ideas, of speech without that of writing, or of writing without that of speech? Are motor residua localized in Broca's convolution, as some physiologists think? We can only suggest these queries, which we are unable to answer. The relation between sign and idea, a simple fact in subjective psychology, becomes in positive psychology a complex problem which can only be solved with a further development of our knowledge of anatomy and physiology.

* *Op. cit.*, p. 156.

Having examined into the nature of amnesia of signs, we have now to study its evolution. I have endeavored to show that it is especially concerned with the motor elements, and have there pointed out its chief characteristic, but whether this hypothesis is admitted or not makes no difference with what is to follow. Sometimes aphasia is of very brief duration. Sometimes it becomes chronic, and, if the patient is seen after the lapse of several years, his condition is not found to be sensibly changed. But there are cases where renewed apoplectic attacks augment the intensity of the disease; it then follows a progressive course which is of the greatest interest to us. Dissolution takes place by stages, so that the memory is effaced more and more in accordance with a regular sequence. This sequence is, 1, words—that is to say, rational language; 2, exclamatory phrases, interjections—what Max Müller calls emotional language; 3, in rare cases, gestures. Let us examine these three periods of dissolution in detail; we shall then have made a comprehensive study of amnesia of signs.

1. The first period is much the most important, since it comprises the higher forms of language, those which are distinctively human, the products of the reasoning, faculties. Here again dissolution follows a determinate order.

Physicians, even prior to contemporary investigation into the mechanism of aphasia, noticed that recollection of proper names is lost before that of substantives, and that the latter in turn precedes the loss of adjectives. This has been confirmed by subsequent observation. "Substantives," says Kussmaul, "and especially proper names and names of things (*Sachnamen*), are more easily forgotten than verbs, adjectives, and other parts of speech." * This fact has only been noted by physicians in a casual way. Very few have sought to discover the causes. It has, in fact, no special interest from a professional point of view, while of great importance in psychology. We see at first glance that the progress of amnesia is from the particular to the general. It first effaces proper names which are purely individual, then the names of concrete things, then substantives not formed from adjectives, and, finally, adjectives and verbs which express qualities, states of being, and acts. Signs directly expressive of quality are the last to disappear. The savant mentioned by Gratiolet, who, having forgotten proper names, said, "My friend who invented" so and so, had reached the stage of designation by qualities. It has also been noted that many idiots have memory only of adjectives (Itard). The notion of quality is the most stable because

* *Op. cit.*, p. 164.

it is the first to be acquired, and because it is the basis of the most complex mental conceptions.

As the particular is necessarily that which has the least extension, and the general that which has the most, we may say that the rapidity with which signs disappear from the memory is in inverse ratio to their extension; and as, other things being equal, a term has more chances of being repeated and fixed in the memory the greater the number of objects it represents, and the least chance of being repeated and fixed in the memory the smaller the number represented, we see that the law of dissolution is definitively supported by experimental conditions. In connection with this subject the following passage from Kussmaul may be read with advantage: "As the memory fails, the more concrete the concept the quicker its corresponding term will disappear. The cause of this is that our representation of persons and things is less firmly associated with their names than with their relative abstract terms, such as apply to their condition, relations, or qualities. We can easily form mental images of persons and things without their names, because the sentient image is more familiar than the other image, the sign—that is to say, the name. On the other hand, we acquire abstract concepts only by the aid of words which give them a stable form. That is why verbs, adjectives, pronouns, and especially adverbs, prepositions, and conjunctions are more firmly fixed in the mind than substantives. We may suppose that in the plexus of cells in the cortex the phenomena of excitation and combination are much more numerous for an abstract concept than for a concrete concept; and, consequently, that the organic connections uniting the abstract idea with its sign are much more numerous than those required in the case of a concrete idea." * Expressed in psychological terms, this last phrase is equivalent to what we said above, viz., that the stability of the sign varies directly as its organization—that is to say, as the number of experiences repeated and registered.

The science of language also provides us with valuable illustrations which I can not ignore, even at the risk of wearying the reader with a superabundance of evidence. The evolution of language takes place, as we would naturally infer, in an inverse order to that of its dissolution in aphasia. But before having recourse to the law of the historical development of language, it would seem reasonable that we should first examine its individual development. This, however, is impossible. When we learn to speak, our language is borrowed. Although a child, as

* *Op. cit.*, p. 164.

M. Taine has well said, "learns a language already made as a musician learns counter-point and a poet prosody, that is to say, as a creative genius," in fact he creates nothing. We are therefore obliged to confine ourselves to historic evolution. It is now well established that the Indo-European languages have their origin in a certain number of roots, and that these roots are of two kinds: verbal or predicative, and pronominal or demonstrative. The first class, comprising verbs, adjectives, and substantives, are, according to Professor Whitney, signs indicative of acts or qualities. The second class, whence come the pronoun and adverb (the preposition and conjunction are of secondary formation), are not so numerous, and indicate relative position. The primitive form of word-signs is, therefore, an affirmation of quality. Then the verb and adjective are differentiated. "Names are derived from verbs by the intermediation of participles, which are simply adjectives, with the verbal derivation effaced." * The transformation of common nouns into proper nouns is plain. Does not the natural evolution of language explain the various stages of its dissolution in aphasia, as far as a spontaneous creation and the decay of a language artifically learned are comparable?

* F. Baudry, "De la science du langage," p. 16. For further details see the works of Max Müller and Professor Whitney.

2. In examining in a general way the law of the regression of memory, we saw that the memory of sensations was effaced after that of ideas. By analogy we are led to the conclusion that in the special case which we are considering—progressive amnesia of signs—the language of the emotions should disappear before the language of reason. This deduction is fully proved by observation.

The best observers (Broca, Trousseau, Hughlings Jackson, Broadbent, etc.) have recorded many instances where victims of aphasia, completely deprived of speech and incapable of articulating a single word voluntarily, were able to utter not only exclamations, but complete phrases in which they expressed anger or spite, or deplored their infirmity. One of the most persistent forms of language under such conditions is that of oaths.

We have remarked in a general way that states of most recent formation are the first to disappear, while the oldest are the last to be effaced. We have here a confirmation: the language of the emotions is formed before the language of ideas; it disappears after. Again, the complex disappears before the simple, and the language of reason compared with that of the sensations is of extreme complexity.

3. The foregoing is applicable to gestures.

This form of language, the most natural of all, is not (like the interjection, for instance) simply a mode of reflex expression. It appears in the child long before articulate language. In certain savage tribes it plays a more important part than spoken words. This innate language is rarely lost. "Those cases of aphasia in which we find imitative disorders are always," says Kussmaul, "of an extremely complex nature. Sometimes the patient realizes that his gestures are deceptive, sometimes he is not conscious of their meaning." * Hughlings Jackson, who has given special attention to this point, notes that in certain cases the patient can neither laugh, nor smile, nor weep, except under stress of great emotion. He also remarks that some affirm or deny by gestures, without discrimination. One who still retained a few interjections and gestures used them in an unintelligible way and in a contrary sense. An instance cited by Trousseau is a remarkable example of purely motor amnesia as affecting gestures. "I held my hands before me and moved my fingers as if I were playing the clarionet, and requested the patient to imitate me. He did so with perfect precision. 'You see,' I said to him, 'I am making the motions of a man who plays the clarionet?' He responded with an affirmation. A few minutes later I asked him to go

* *Op. cit.*, p. 160.

through the same movements. He reflected for a time, but was entirely unable to reproduce a mimicry so simple."

Reviewing what we have gone over in this section, we see that amnesia of signs progresses from proper names to substantives, then to adjectives and verbs, then to the language of the emotions, and finally to gestures. This destructive movement does not take place at random; it is governed by a rigorous principle—from the least organized to the most organized, from complex to simple, from the least automatic to the most automatic.* What has been said above with regard to the general law of reversion of memory might be repeated here, and it is not one of the least significant proofs of its exactitude that it should be verified in cases of partial amnesia, the most important, the most systematic, and the best known of all affections of the memory. There is still space for a counter-proof. When amnesia of signs is complete and recovery begins, do they return in inverse order to that in which they disappeared? Illustrations are rare. I find, however, a case recorded by Dr. Grasset of a man who was seized with "complete inability of expressing his thoughts either by speech, by writing, or by gestures. After a time the faculty of

* It is a remarkable fact that many subjects of aphasia who are unable to write are still capable of signing their names.

expression returned little by little, first manifesting itself through gestures, then through speech and writing." * It is probable that other examples of this kind might be found if special attention were given to the subject by qualified observers.

* "Revue des sciences médicales," etc., 1873, t. ii, p. 684.

CHAPTER IV.

EXALTATIONS OF MEMORY, OR HYPERMNESIA.

UP to this point our pathological study has been limited to forms destructive of memory; we have thus seen its diminution or effacement. But there are cases entirely opposite in character, where functions that were apparently obliterated are revived, and vague recollections attain to extraordinary intensity. Is this exaltation of memory, which physicians term hypermnesia, a morbid phenomenon? It is, at least, an anomaly. And, as it is always associated with some organic disorder, or with some curious or unusual condition, there can be no doubt that it comes within the province of this work. Its study is less instructive than that of amnesia, but a monograph should neglect nothing that may throw light upon the subject in hand. We shall see, moreover, that it teaches us something with regard to the persistence of recollections.

Excitations of memory are general or partial.

I.

General excitation of memory is difficult to define, since the degree of excitation is entirely relative. It would be necessary to compare memory with memory as existing in the same person. The power of memory varying with the individual, there is no common measure; amnesia with one may be hypermnesia in another. It is, in fact, a change of *tone* produced in the memory as in all other forms of psychical activity, thought, imagination, sensibility. Moreover, when we say that excitation is general, we only state a reasonable induction. As memory is subject to the condition of consciousness, and as consciousness is only evolved in the form of a succession, all that we can say is that, during a greater or less period of time, a multitude of recollections spring up on every side. General excitation of memory seems to depend entirely upon physiological causes, and particularly upon the rapidity of the cerebral circulation. Hence, it frequently appears in acute fevers. It is still more common in maniacal excitation, in ecstasy, in hypnotism; sometimes it appears in hysteria and in the early stages of certain diseases of the brain.

Aside from these cases which are distinctively pathological, there are others of a more extraordinary nature, which probably arise from the same cause. There are several accounts of drowned persons saved from imminent death who agree that at the moment of asphyxia they seemed to see their entire lives unrolled before them in the minutest incidents. One of them testifies that "every instance of his former life seemed to glance across his recollection in a retrograde succession, not in mere outline, but the picture being filled with every minute and collateral feature," forming "a kind of panoramic picture of his entire existence, each act of it accompanied by a sense of right and wrong." An analogous case is that of "a man of remarkably clear head," who "was crossing a railway in the country when an express train at full speed appeared closely approaching him. He had just time to throw himself down in the center of the road between the two lines of rails, and as the vast train passed over him, the sentiment of impending danger to his very existence brought vividly into his recollection every incident of his former life in such an array as that which is suggested by the promised opening of 'the great book at the last great day.'"* Even allowing for exaggeration, these instances show a superintensity of action on the part of the memory of which we can have no idea in its normal state.

* For these cases, and others of like nature, see Forbes Winslow, *op. cit.*, p. 303, *et seq.*

I shall cite a final illustration of exaltation of memory due to intoxication from the use of opium, and request the reader to note in what manner it confirms the explanation given above with regard to the mechanism of recollection. "Sometimes," writes De Quincey in his "Confessions of an English Opium-Eater," "sometimes I seemed to have lived for seventy or a hundred years in one night. . . . The minutest incidents of childhood, or forgotten scenes of later years, were often revived. I could not be said to recollect them; for, if I had been told of them when waking, I should not have been able to acknowledge them as parts of my past experience. But, placed as they were before me, in dreams like intuitions, and clothed in all their evanescent circumstances and accompanying feelings, I recognized them instantaneously" (p. 259).

All general excitations of memory are transitory; they never survive the inducing causes. Are there cases of permanent hypermnesia? If the term is made to assume a slightly forced meaning, it may be applied to the singular development of memory that sometimes follows certain injuries. Upon this point plenty of oft-repeated stories may be found in old writers (Clement VI, Mabillon, etc.). These statements may be accepted as true, for modern observers, Romberg among others, have noted a remarkable and permanent development of memory after shocks, attacks of small-pox, etc. The mechanism of this metamorphosis being inscrutable, there is no reason why we should dwell upon it here.

II.

Partial excitation is from its nature fixed within definite limits. The ordinary tone of the memory being generally maintained, special development of any form is very noticeable. Hypermnesia of this kind is the necessary correlative of partial amnesia; it proves once more and in another way that the memory is made up of memories. In the evolution of partial hypermnesia no law is discernible. Each case presents itself as an isolated fact—that is to say, as the resultant of certain conditions which we are unable to determine. Why should a certain group of cells forming a given dynamical association be spurred into action more than any other? We can give no reason, either physiological or psychological. The only cases where there would seem to be any trace of a law are those mentioned in the following pages where several languages returned successively to the memory. Partial excitation nearly always results from morbid causes indicated above; but it sometimes occurs in a state of health, as will be seen from the two examples following:—

"A lady, in the last stage of a chronic disease, was carried from London to a lodging in the country; there her infant daughter was taken to visit her, and, after a short interview, carried back to town. The lady died a few days after, and the daughter grew up without any recollection of her mother till she was of mature age. At this time she happened to be taken into the room in which her mother died, without knowing it to have been so; she started on entering it, and, when a friend who was along with her asked the cause of her agitation, she replied: 'I have a distinct impression of having been in this room before, and that a lady, who lay in that corner, and seemed very ill, leaned over me and wept.'" *

A clergyman endowed with a decidedly artistic temperament (a fact worth noting) went with a party of friends to a castle in Sussex, which he did not remember ever to have previously visited. "As he approached the gateway, he became conscious of a very vivid impression of having seen it before; and he 'seemed to himself to see' not only the gateway itself, but donkeys beneath the arch, and people on the top of it. His conviction that he *must* have visited the castle on some former occasion made him inquire from his mother if she could throw any light on the matter. She at once informed him that, be-

* Abercrombie, "Essay on the Intellectual Powers," p. 120.

ing in that part of the country when he was about *eighteen months* old, she had gone over with a large party, and taken him in the pannier of a donkey; that the elders of the party, having brought lunch with them, had eaten it on the roof of the gateway where they would have been seen from below, while he had been left on the ground with the attendants and donkeys." *

The mechanism of recollection in these two cases leaves no room for misunderstanding. There was in each instance revivification by contiguity in space. These examples only present in a more striking and less common form what is constantly occurring every day of our lives. Who has not, in order to recover an impression momentarily lost, made his way to the spot where the idea first arose in order to place himself as far as possible in the same material situation, and at length find it suddenly revived? As to hypermnesia from morbid causes, I shall give but one example which may serve as a type:

"A case has been related to me," says Abercrombie, "of a boy who at the age of four received a fracture of the skull, for which he underwent the operation of trepan. He was at the time in a state of perfect stupor, and after his recovery retained no recollection either of the accident or of the operation. At the age of fif-

* Carpenter, *op. cit.*, p. 431.

teen, during the delirium of a fever, he gave his mother a correct description of the operation, and the persons who were present at it, with their dress and other minute particulars. He had never been observed to allude to it before, and no means were known by which he could have acquired the circumstances which he mentioned." *

The complete recovery of a forgotten language merits attention. The case reported by Coleridge is well known, and there are many others of the same kind to be found in the works of Abercrombie, Hamilton, and Carpenter. The anæsthetic sleep induced by chloroform or ether sometimes produces the same effects as does febrile excitation. "An old forester had lived in his boyhood on the frontier of Poland, where he had never spoken anything but the Polish tongue. Afterward he lived in the German districts, and his children assert that for thirty or forty years he neither heard nor pronounced a single Polish word. During an attack of anæsthesia which lasted nearly two hours, he spoke, prayed, and sang, using only the Polish language." †

More curious than the return of one language is the progressive return of several languages. Unfortunately, authors who have reported facts

* *Op. cit.*, p. 149.

† Duval, "Nouveau dict. de médecine," article "Hypnotisme," p. 144.

of this kind speak of them as simple curiosities without giving the information necessary for their interpretation. The most clearly described case is recorded by Dr. Rush, of Philadelphia. "Dr. Scandella, an ingenious Italian, who visited this country a few years ago, was master of the Italian, French, and English languages. In the beginning of the yellow fever, which terminated his life, . . . he spoke English only; in the middle of the disease, he spoke French only; but, on the day of his death, he spoke only in the language of his native country."* The same author speaks in a very confusing way of a woman subject to attacks of temporary insanity. At first she spoke bad Italian; at the most acute period of the disease, French; during the subsidence of the attack, German; and, when she had entered upon the road to convalescence, she returned to her mother-tongue, English. Setting aside regression through several languages for more simple cases, we find illustrations in abundance. A Frenchman living in England, speaking English perfectly, received a blow on the head. During the illness that followed he was only able to reply to questions in French. But there is no observation more instructive than the following, also reported by Dr. Rush. He knew, he tells us, a

* "Medical Inquiries and Observations upon Diseases of the Mind," p. 277.

German, for many years minister of the Lutheran Church in Philadelphia, "who, in visiting the old Swedes who inhabited the southern district of the city, upon their death-beds, was much struck in hearing some of them pray in the Swedish language, who he was sure had not spoken it for fifty or sixty years before, and who had probably forgotten it." * Forbes Winslow also notes a case of a physician who had in early life renounced the principles of the Roman Catholic Church, and who, during an attack of delirium preceding his death, prayed only in the forms of the Church of Rome, all recollection of the prescribed formulæ of the Protestant religion being obliterated.†

This return of languages and forgotten phrases seems to me, when properly interpreted, to be only a particular case of the law of regression. In the progress of a morbid action which nearly always ends in death, the most recent formations of memory are first destroyed, and the destructive work goes on, descending, so to speak, from layer to layer, until it reaches the oldest acquisitions—that is to say, the most stable—incites them to temporary activity, brings them for a time into consciousness, and then wipes them out for ever. Hypermnesia would then be only the result of

* *Op. cit.*, *ibid.*

† *Op. cit.*, p. 266. [Chapter xv, on "Chronic Affections of the Memory," contains many interesting illustrations.—Tr.]

conditions entirely negative; regression would result, not from a normal return to consciousness, but from the suppression of more active and more intense states, like a weak voice that could only make itself heard when more powerful organs of speech had relapsed into silence. These acquisitions of infancy and youth come into prominence, not because of some ulterior force pushing them out from their environment, but because there is nothing left to interfere with their freedom of action. Revivifications of this kind are, strictly speaking, only a return to pristine vigor, to conditions of existence which had apparently disappeared for ever, but which the retrograde work of dissolution brings again into operation. I shall abstain from reflections naturally suggested by these facts, leaving such themes to the moralists. Perhaps they will be able to explain how certain religious ecstacies manifested in last moments are in the view of psychology only the necessary effects of irremediable dissolution. Independently of this unexpected confirmation of the law of regression, another notable fact in the study of hypermnesia is the surprising persistence of those latent conditions of recollection which are termed residua. If it were not for the diseases of memory, we should never suspect their existence; for consciousness left to itself can only affirm the conservation of states that go to make up the current of life, and of a few others dependent on the will and fixed by habit.

Must we infer from these revivifications that absolutely nothing is lost upon the memory? that when a perception or impression has once entered there it is indestructible? that even the most fleeting impression may be at any moment revived? Many authorities, particularly Maury, have supported these queries with striking illustrations. However, if any one chooses to maintain that, even without the assistance of morbid causes, residua sometimes disappear, there are no means of disproving the assertion.* It is possible that certain cellular modifications and dynamic associations are too unstable to last. But we may at least say that persistence, if not absolute, is the general rule, and that it includes an immense majority of cases. As to the method by which these distant recollections are conserved and reproduced we know nothing. I can only explain how the hypothesis adopted throughout this work may be applied here.

If we assume cellular modifications and dynamic associations as the material basis of recollection, there is no memory, it matters not how crowded it may be, that is not able to retain all that comes within its grasp, for, if possible cellu-

* See article by M. Delbœuf in the "Revue Philosophique," February 1, 1880.

lar modifications are limited, the possible dynamic associations are innumerable. We may suppose that the old associations reappear when the new, temporarily disorganized, leave the field free. The possible number of revivifications being greatly diminished, the chances are proportionately increased for the return of the most stable—that is to say, the longest-formed—associations. But I can not dwell upon a hypothesis incapable of proof, since my purpose is to keep within the boundaries of positive knowledge.

There is an illusion of a curious nature that can not be referred to any of the morbid types which precede. It is not of frequent occurrence, or at least is rarely observed, only three or four cases being known, and it has not yet received any particular designation. Wigan calls it, improperly, double consciousness; Sander, an illusion of memory (*Erinnerungstauschung*). Others have given it the name of pseudo-memory, which seems to me to be preferable to either of the foregoing. It consists in the belief that a new state has been previously experienced, so that when produced for the first time it seems to be a repetition. Wigan, in his well-known work on "Duality of the Mind," tells us that when present at the funeral of the Princess Charlotte, in Windsor Chapel, he suddenly had the conviction that he had witnessed the same scenes somewhere before. This illusion was momentary, but there are instances of others more durable. Lewes associates the phenomenon with other illusions of more frequent occurrence. Sometimes in a strange region a sudden turn in the road brings us face to face with a landscape which we seem to have beheld before. Coming into the presence of a person for the first time, we *feel* as if we had already seen him. Reading a book with which we are unfamiliar, the thoughts and the language appear as if they had been previously presented to the mind.*

The illusion is easily explained. The received impression evokes analogous impressions in the past, vague, confused, and scarcely tangible, but sufficiently distinct to induce the belief that the new state is a repetition. There is a basis of resemblance between two states of consciousness which is readily perceived and which leads to an imaginary identification. It is an error, but only in part, since there is really in the recorded impressions of the past something resembling a first experience. If this explanation is sufficient for very simple cases, there are others where it is inadmissible.

An invalid, Sander tells us, upon learning of the death of a person whom he knew, was seized

* Lewes, *op. cit.*, third series, p. 129.

with an undefinable terror, because it seemed to him that he knew of the event before. "It seemed to me that some time previous, while I was lying here in this same bed, X. came to me and said, 'Müller is dead.' I replied, 'Müller has been dead for some time; he can not die twice.'"*

Dr. Arnold Pick reports a case of pseudo-memory the most complete within my knowledge. The disorder assumed an almost chronic form. An educated man, who seems to have understood his disease, and who himself gave a written description of it, was seized at the age of thirty-two with a singular mental affection. If he was present at a social gathering, if he visited any place whatever, if he met a stranger, the incident, with all the attendant circumstances, appeared so familiar that he was convinced of having received the same impressions before, of having been surrounded by the same persons or the same objects, under the same sky and the same state of the weather. If he undertook any new occupation, he seemed to have gone through with it at some previous time and under the same conditions. The feeling sometimes appeared the same day, at the end of a few moments or hours, sometimes not till the following day, but always with perfect distinctness.†

* Sander, "Archiv für Psychiatrie," 1873, iv.

"Archiv für Psychiatrie," 1876, vi, 2.

In this phenomenon of pseudo-memory there is an anomalous condition of the mental mechanism which eludes investigation and which is difficult to understand in a state of health. The patient, even if he were a good observer, could not analyze his symptoms without ceasing to be a dupe. It would appear from the examples given that the received impression is reproduced in the form of an image (in physiological terms, there is a repetition of the primitive cerebral process). There is nothing extraordinary in this; it occurs in the case of all recollection not stimulated by the actual presence of the object. The whole difficulty lies in determining in what manner the image, formed a minute, an hour, a day after the real state, gives to the latter the character of a repetition. It may be assumed that the mechanism of recollection, or localization in time, acts in a retrograde manner. For my part I prefer the explanation following.

The image, formed as intimated above, is very intense and of the nature of a hallucination; it imposes itself upon the mind as a reality because there is nothing by which the illusion may be rectified. Hence, the real impression is relegated to a secondary place as a recollection; it is localized in the past, wrongly if the facts are considered in an objective sense, rightly if we take the subjective view. This illusory state, although very active, does not efface the real impression, but, as it is detached from it, as it is produced by it, it appears as a second experience. It takes the place of the real impression, it appears to be the most recent; is so, in fact. To us, judging from the outside, the idea that the impression has been twice received is scouted as absurd. To the patient, judging from the testimony of consciousness, it is true that the impression has been received twice, and within these limits his affirmation is incontestable. In support of this explanation, it may be well to note that pseudo-memory is nearly always associated with mental disorder. Dr. Pick's case ended in a form of insanity, the delirium of fancied persecution. The formation of illusory images is, therefore, perfectly natural. I do not pretend, however, that my theory is the only one possible. For a state so unusual more and better observations are necessary.*

* If we have said nothing with regard to the condition of memory in insanity it is because that collective term designates very different states, of which the most important have been mentioned in the proper place (mania, general paralysis, dementia, etc.). It may be of service to the reader, however, if his attention is called to the following passage from Griesinger, which covers the subject in a general way. "As to memory," he says, "it presents three notable differences in the insane. Sometimes it is perfectly faithful, for events of early life as well as for those which have occurred during disease. More often it is weak in some respects; this is especially the case in dementia. In other cases incidents of the former life are either completely effaced from the memory (which is very rare), or they are referred to

such a distance (and this is more frequent) as to become so vague and strange that the patient is scarcely able to recognize them as having come within the range of his experience. . . .

"A person cured of insanity ordinarily remembers events which happened during the progress of the disease, and is often able to recount with surprising fidelity and precision the minutest incidents that took place, and to explain in detail the motives and mental disposition that governed his actions. He is also often able to describe every gesture, tone, and change of countenance in those who visited him. This is particularly noticeable in persons cured of melancholia or the less pronounced forms of mania; less so in monomania, when the patient's recollections are usually much confused. When a recovered patient declares that he is unable to remember what took place during his insanity, the assertion should be accepted with reserve, since shame often keeps him silent." ("Treatise on Mental Diseases.") See, also, Maudsley in "Reynolds's System of Medicine," v. ii, p. 26. The weakness of the memory in drunkenness is well known. There are many examples of violent acts committed in this state of which no recollection remained. Chronic alcoholism impoverishes the memory without effacing it altogether; in its final stages it develops into dementia and amnesia.

CHAPTER V.

CONCLUSION.

To describe the various diseases of memory, and to seek to determine the law which governs their evolution, has been our endeavor up to this point. In conclusion, something should be said with regard to causes — of immediate organic causes, that is. Even when reduced to these terms, the etiology of diseases of memory is very obscure, and what is definitely known concerning it may be stated in very brief space. Memory consists of a conservation and a reproduction: conservation seems to depend especially upon nutrition; reproduction upon general or local circulation.

I.

Conservation, which is, on the whole, the more important of these two functions, since without it reproduction is impossible, supposes a primary condition that can only be expressed in the vague phraseology, "a normal constitution of the brain." We have seen that idiots are the subjects of congenital amnesia, of an innate inability to fix impressions. This first condition is, therefore, a postulate; it is less a condition of memory than an essential condition of the existence of memory. It is found, in fact, in all persons of a healthy mental state. This normal constitution being granted, it is not enough that impressions be received; they must be fixed, organically registered, conserved; they must produce permanent modifications in the brain; the modifications impressed upon the nerve-cells and -filaments, and the dynamic associations which these elements form must be stable. This result can depend only on nutrition. The brain, and particularly the gray substance, receives an enormous amount of blood. There is no portion of the body where the work of nutrition is more complete or more rapid. We are ignorant of the special mechanism of this work. Histology can not follow molecular changes. We can only observe effects; all the rest is hypothesis. But there are facts enough to prove the direct relation between nutrition and the memory.

That children learn with marvelous facility, and that everthing depending upon memory, such as the acquirement of a language, is easily mastered by them, is a matter of common observation. We also know that habits (a certain form of memory) are more readily acquired in childhood and youth than in after-life. At the former period the activity of the processes of nutrition is so great that new associations are rapidly established. In the aged, on the contrary, the prompt effacement of new impressions coincides with a notable diminution of this activity. What is quickly learned is soon forgotten. The expression "to assimilate knowledge" is not a metaphor. The psychical fact has an organic cause. For the fixation of recollections, time is necessary, since nutrition does not do its work in a moment; the incessant molecular movement of which it is composed must follow a constant path in order that an impression periodically renewed may be maintained.*

* "A distinguished theatrical performer," says Abercrombie, "in consequence of the sudden illness of another actor, had occasion to prepare himself, on very short notice, for a part which was entirely new to him; and the part was long and rather difficult. He acquired it in a very short time, and went through it with perfect accuracy, but immediately after the performance forgot every word of it. Characters which he had acquired in a more deliberate manner he never forgets, but can perform them at any time without a moment's preparation; but, in regard to the character now mentioned, there was the further and very singular fact that, though he has repeatedly performed it since that time, he has been obliged each time to prepare it anew, and has never acquired in regard to it that facility which is familiar to him in other instances. When questioned respecting the mental process which he employed the first time he performed this part, he says that he lost sight entirely of the audience, and seemed to have nothing before him but the pages of the book from which he had learned it; and, that if anything had occurred to interrupt the illusion, he should have stopped instantly." (*Op. cit.*, p. 103.)

Fatigue in any form is fatal to memory. The received impressions are not fixed; reproduction is slow, often impossible. Fatigue is a result of superactivity in an organ by which nutrition suffers and languishes. With a return to normal conditions memory returns. The incident related by Holland, cited in a previous chapter, offers explicit testimony upon this point. We have also seen that, in cases where amnesia follows cerebral shock, forgetfulness is always retrograde, extending over a more or less protracted period, previous to the accident. Most physiologists who have given attention to this phenomenon explain it as resulting from defective nutrition. Organic registration, which consists in a nutritive modification of the cerebral substance, is for some reason wanting. Finally, it should be remembered that disease of memory in its gravest form—progressive amnesia of dementia, old age, or general paralysis—is caused by an increasing atrophy of the nervous elements. The capillaries and cells undergo degeneration; the latter finally disappear, leaving in their place only ineffective *débris*.

These facts—physiological and pathological—show that there is between nutrition and conservation the relation of cause and effect. There is an exact coincidence in the periods of culmination and decline. Variations, short or long, in one, have corresponding variations in the other.

If one be active, or moderate, or languishing, the other is similarly affected. Conservation of impressions must, therefore, be conceived not in a metaphysical sense as "a faculty of the mind," existing no one knows where, but as an acquired state of the cerebral organism which implies the possibility of conscious states when their conditions of existence are fulfilled. The extreme rapidity of nutritive changes in the brain, which at first thought would seem to be a source of instability, is in reality the cause of the fixation of recollections.

"The waste following activity is restored by nutrition, and a trace or residuum remains embodied in the constitution of the nervous center, becoming more complete and distinct with each succeeding repetition of the impression; an acquired nature is grafted on the original nature of the cell by virtue of its plastic power."* We here touch the primal meaning of memory as a biological fact: it is an impregnation. Hence it is not surprising that the eminent English surgeon, Sir James Paget, in treating of the permanent modifications made in the living tissues by contagious diseases, should express himself in the following terms, particularly applicable to our discussion: "It is asked," he says, "how can the brain be the organ of memory when you

* Maudsley, "Physiology and Pathology of the Mind," p. 91.

suppose its substance to be ever changing? or how is it that your assumed nutritive change of all the particles of the brain is not as destructive of all memory and knowledge of sensuous things as the sudden destruction by some great injury is? The answer is, because of the exactness of assimilation accomplished in the formative process: the effect once produced by an impression upon the brain, whether in perception or in intellectual act, is fixed and there retained; because the part, be it what it may, which has been thereby changed, is exactly represented in the part which, in the course of nutrition, succeeds to it." * Paradoxical as it may appear, the connection between contagious diseases and the memory is, from a biological point of view, rigorously exact.

II.

In a general way, reproduction of impressions seems to depend upon the circulation. It is a problem much more obscure than the preceding, and concerning which we have very incomplete data. The first difficulty arises from the rapidity of action and change; the second from the complexity of those functions. Reproduction, moreover, does not depend entirely upon the general circulation; it is dependent upon the circumscribed circulation in the brain, and here again

* "Lectures on Surgical Pathology," p. 58.

there are probably local variations of great influence. Nor is this all: we must also consider the *quality* of the blood as well as its *quantity*. It is impossible to determine, even in a general way, the importance of each of these factors in the mechanism of reproduction. We can only point out that the circulation and the reproduction of impressions have correlative variations. The facts supporting this view are as follows:

Fever, in its various stages, is accompanied by extreme cerebral activity. In this activity the memory participates. We have even seen at what point of excitation it may be effaced. It is known that in fever the rapidity of the circulation is excessive, that the blood is altered from its normal state, and that it is charged with the waste products arising from too rapid combustion. This variation in quality and quantity finds its psychological expression in hypermnesia. But, aside from a febrile state, "impressions of trivial things, in which no particular interest was taken, often survive in memory when impressions of much more important or imposing things fade away; and, on considering the circumstances, it will frequently be found that such impressions were received when the energies were high—when exercise, or pleasure, or both, had greatly raised the action of the heart. That at times, when strong emotion has excited the circulation to an exceptional degree, the clustered sensations yielded by surrounding objects are revivable with great clearness, often throughout life, is a fact noted by writers of fiction as a trait of human nature." * We may note again the ease and rapidity with which reproduction takes place at that period of life when the blood is driven through the veins in plentiful and swift-moving streams, and how slow and difficult it becomes when the circulation diminishes with advancing years. It is also noticeable that in the latter part of life the composition of the blood is changed, it being less rich in red corpuscles and albumen. In those exhausted by long illnesses memory is enfeebled with the circulation. "Highly nervous subjects, too, in whom the action of the heart is greatly lowered, habitually complain of loss of memory and inability to think—symptoms which diminish as fast as the natural rate of circulation is regained." †

Exaltation of the memory ensues when the circulation is increased by stimulants, such as hasheesh, opium, etc., which excite the nervous system and then leave it in a state of depression. Other therapeutic agents induce a contrary effect,

* Spencer, "Principles of Psychology," v. i, p. 235.

† Spencer, *op. cit.*, v. i, p. 237.

bromide of potassium, for example, which is sedative or hypnotic in its action, and, taken in large doses, retards the circulation. A clergyman was obliged to discontinue its use; he had very nearly lost his memory, which returned when the medicine was suspended.

From a consideration of all these facts we reach a general conclusion: a normal exercise of the memory supposes an active circulation, and blood rich in the materials necessary for integration and disintegration. When this activity is unduly increased, there is a tendency toward morbid excitation; when it decreases, there is a tendency toward amnesia. We can push our conclusions no further without entering the domain of pure hypothesis. Why is a given group of recollections revived or effaced in preference to any other? We do not know. There is so much that is uncertain in every case of amnesia or hypermnesia that it would be vain to attempt an explanation. It is probable that transitory organic modifications arising from infinitesimal causes are the inducing agents by which one series is called into action and another repressed. If a single nervous element is destroyed or paralyzed, that suffices; the well-known mechanism of association will explain the rest. Some physiologists have advanced the theory that limited and temporary lapses of memory are due to local and transient modifications in the caliber of the arteries under the influence of the vaso-motor nerves. The reason for this view is that the return of mental power is sudden and is ordinarily induced by strong emotion, and that the emotions exercise a particular sway over the vaso-motor system. In cases of complete loss of memory, of which we have given many examples, return depends upon the circulation and nutrition. If sudden, which rarely happens, the most probable hypothesis is that the cause was a suspended function, a state of inhibition, which was abruptly terminated; this problem is one of the most obscure in the physiology of the nervous system. If recovery result from re-education (as it ordinarily does), the chief part devolves upon nutrition. The rapidity with which the patient learns shows that all was not lost. The cells may have been atrophied; but, if their *nuclei* (generally considered as the seat of reproduction) give origin to other cells, the bases of memory are re-established; the new cells resemble the parent-cells by virtue of that tendency of every organism to maintain its type, and of every acquired modification to transmit its characteristics to succeeding forms; memory in this case is only a phase of heredity.*

* For details, see "Brain," articles cited in ch. ii, § 1.

III.

To sum up, memory is a general function of the nervous system. It is based upon the faculty possessed by the nervous elements of conserving a received modification and of forming associations. These associations, the result of experience, we have styled dynamic, to distinguish them from natural or anatomical associations. Conservation is assured by nutrition, which is always recording because always renewed. The power of reproduction depends, above all, upon the circulation. Conservation and reproduction: all that is essential to memory is thus united with the fundamental conditions of life. The rest—consciousness, localization in the past—is only superadded. Psychical memory is nothing but the highest and most complex form of organic memory. If we limit investigation to that, as many psychologists have done, we condemn ourselves in advance to the pursuit of mere abstractions. These preliminary propositions established, we have classified and described the diseases of memory; and, as special observation is of greater service, more instructive and suggestive, than a general description, we have given of each morbid type clear and authentic examples. Having passed in review a long series of observations, we have sought to formulate certain general conclusions. In the first place, we have shown the necessity of resolving memory into *memories*, the independence of each form being clearly established by morbid cases. We then demonstrated that dissolution of memory followed a law. Setting aside secondary disorders of brief duration which throw very little light upon those which are normal in their method of evolution, we have arrived at the following conclusions:

1. In cases of general dissolution of the memory, loss of recollections follows an invariable path: recent events, ideas in general, feelings, and acts.

2. In the best-known cases of partial dissolution (forgetfulness of signs), loss of recollection follows an invariable path: proper names, common nouns, adjectives and verbs, interjections, gestures.

3. In each of these classes the destructive process is identical. It is a regression from the new to the old, from the complex to the simple, from the voluntary to the automatic, from the least organized to the best organized.

4. The exactitude of the *law of regression* is verified in those rare cases where progressive dissolution of the memory is followed by recovery; recollections return in an inverse order to that in which they disappear.

5. This law of regression provides us with an

explanation for extraordinary revivification of certain recollections when the mind turns backward to conditions of existence that had apparently disappeared for ever.

6. We have founded this law upon this physiological principle: Degeneration first affects what has been most recently formed; and upon this psychological principle: The complex disappears before the simple, because it has not been repeated so often in experience.

Finally, our pathological study has led us to this general conclusion: Memory consists of a process of organization of variable stages between two extreme limits—the new state, the organic registration.

INDEX.

Abercrombie, 181.
Abstract concepts, memory of, 167.
Acoustic memory, 159, 163.
Adjectives, memory of, 168.
Adverbs, memory of, 168.
Agraphia, 152.
Amnesia, 70; temporary, 71; periodical, 71; progressive, 71; congenital, 71, 131; temporary, of a destructive character, 79; instances of, requiring re-education, 82–94; total, 95; proportioned to degree of organization, 95, 172; physiological cause of, 96; complete, 97; movement of, governed by natural forces, 122; partial, meaning of, 138; of signs, 151; theory of amnesia of signs, 155, 160; progress of amnesia of signs, 172.
Amnesia of signs, a disease of the motor memory, 154.
Analogies of memory, 11, 12.
Anatomical cause of failing memory, 120.
Anatomical lesion the cause of dementia, 118.
Aphasia, 151; varieties of, 152; chronic, 160.
Apple, analysis of the memory of, 42.
Automatic functions the last to disappear, 127.
Automatic movements, how acquired, 15; localizations become automatic, 52.
Automatism, mental, 72.
Azam, Dr., 99, 101, 102, 104.

Baillarger, 118, 120.
Bain, Alexander, 162.
Beattie, Dr., 144.
Biological memory, 66.
Broadbent, 170.
Broca, 170.
Broca's convolution, motor residua localized in, 164.
Bromide of potassium, 200.
Brown-Séquard, 96, 161.

Carpenter, 147, 181.
Circulation of the blood and memory, 197.
Classification of diseases of memory, difficulty of, 70.
Clifford, 11.
Cœnæsthesis, 108–112; cause of variations of the, 113; how to determine forms of the, 113.

Colburn, Zerah, 137.
Coleridge, 181.
Combe, 105.
Complexity of the simplest mental functions, 145.
Concrete concepts, memory of, 167.
Congenital amnesia, 71, 131; exceptions in, 134.
Conjunctions, memory of, 168.
Consciousness, an adjunct of nervous processes, 11; in epileptic amnesia, 74; nature of, 78; double, 98; mechanism of, 107; form of, 110; extent of, 11; wanting in organic memory, 18; its relation to unconsciousness, 32; conditions of its existence, 33; its relation to organization, 63, 64.

Degree of organization, stability of memory depens upon, 96.
Dementia, 117.
De Quincey, 177.
Destructive temporary amnesia, 79; examples of, 80.
Diseases of memory, classification of, 70; partial, 70; general, 70; immediate causes of, 192.
Dissolution of memory, law of, 117; course of, in aphasia, 165, 169, 183–186.
Doré, Gustave, 137.
Double memory of words, 163.
Dreams, 76; why forgotten, 77, 88.
Dufay, Dr., 102, 103, 106.
Dunn, 97.
Duration a condition of consciousness, 33; ideas of, 59.
Dynamical associations, 41, 44, 66.

Ego, nature of the, 98, 107–112; unity of, 110, 114.
Emotions slowly effaced, 120; disappearance of the language of, 170.
Epilepsy, and temporary amnesia, 71; psychology of, 73.
Epileptic amnesia, psychological interpretation of, 73.
Epileptic vertigo, 71, 72.
Epileptics, mental state of, 73–79.
Euphrasia of the dying, 109.
Evolution of amnesia of signs, 165.
Evolution of language, order of, 168; explains its dissolution in aphasia, 169.
Excitation of memory, general, 175; partial, 178; cases of, 179.
Expression, complexity of the faculty of, 159.
Extension, its relation to memory, 167.

Fabret, 118.
Facts, the most extraordinary not the most instructive, 69.
Faculties, mental, 141; memory as a faculty, 11.
Faculty of expression, complexity of, 159.
Fatigue and memory, 195.
Feelings, persistence of, 120.
Fever, excitation of memory in, 198.
Forgetfulness, a condition of memory, 61; nature of, 161.
Foville, 118.
Functions, new, how acquired, 13.

Gall, 137.
General disorders of memory, 71.
Gestures, loss of language of, 171.
Granville, 82, 95.
Grasset, Dr., 172.

Gratiolet, 166.
Griesinger, 118, 120.

Hamilton, 105, 181.
Hashecsh, 199.
Hemiplegia, 152.
Hereditary memory, 65.
Hering, 13.
Heterophasia, 152.
Holland, Sir Henry, 144, 195.
Huxley, 11.
Hypermnesia, 175, 178; cases of partial, 179; produced by chloroform, 181.
Hypotheses, need of, 19.
Hypothesis of partial amnesia, 138–142.
Hypothesis, of the production of organic memory, 22–31; concerning the cause of progressive amnesia, 128–131.
Hypothetical explanation of partial memory and of inequalities of memory in the same person, 138–142.

Idiots, 131–134; memory of, 166.
Illusion, all memory an, 47, 58–62.
Imbeciles, senses of, 132.
Imitative disorders, 171.
Indo-European languages, roots of, 169.
Inhibition, 98.
Intensity a condition of consciousness, 33, 75–79.
Ivanhoe, 56.

Jackson, Hughlings, Dr., 72, 75, 78, 127, 170, 171.

Knowledge, how distinguished from feeling, 120.
Kussmaul, 153, note, 162, 167, 171.

Language, loss of, 151; historic evolution of, 168, 169; evolution of, in individual, 168.
Languages, recovery of forgotten, 181–183.
Latent memory, 97.
Law of regression or reversion, 122, 128.
Learning to write, process of, 159.
Lewes, 15, 29, 136, 187.
Linnæus, 55.
Localization of memory, 141, 142; in time, 46; how determined, 49, 50; use of reference points in, 52; in the future, 53; stages of, 55; instances of its absence, 55–57; never instantaneous, 58; disappears, 63.
Locomotion is a secondary automatic function, 14; organization of, 21.
Loss of memory of languages, 144; of music, 144; instances of, 145; of proper names, 145; of numbers, 146.
Louyer-Villermay, 123, 147.

Macario, 104.
Macaulay, 57.
Macnish, 104, 105.
Maudsley, 11, 34, 108.
Maury, 185.
Mechanical work, memory of, 95.
Memory, old idea of, 9; is essentially a biological fact, 10; perfect, 10; bases of, 12; is a product of heredity, 14; seat of, 20; physiological conditions of, 21; implies time, 48; its highest form, 58; forgetfulness a condition of, 61; a morphology, 62; hereditary, 65; depends upon nutrition,

67, 193–197; motor, 154, 159; acoustic, 159; visual, 159, 160; nature of, 161; case of disruption of, 99, 100; nature of double, 106; loss of, 116–122; its most lasting form, 130; law of its progressive destruction, 121; order of its re-establishment, 123–127; import of the word, 136; inequalities of, 136; causes of, 137; varieties of, 135; of an apple, analysis of, 42; of a word, analysis of, 43; general excitation of, 175; partial excitation of, 178; fatigue in, 195.
Mental activity in amnesia of signs, cases of, 157.
Mental automatism, 72; instances of, 72; psychology of, 73; consciousness in, 74.
Mental disease, early indications of, 109.
Morel, 73.
Motor amnesia, 155–165; as affecting gestures, 171.
Motor memory, 154.
Motor residua, 155–159.
Mozart, 137.
Müller, Max, 165.

Names, why forgotten before abstract terms, 167; how derived, 169.
Natural classification of mental diseases, 70.
Nerve cells, 24, 27, 38, 67.
Nervous discharges, 38.
Nervous system: its relation to consciousness, 32; to reflex consciousness, 35.
Nervous tissue, 14, 67.
Newton, 55.
Nutrition and memory, 193, 197.

Ogle, W., 164.
Order of intensity of mental states, 77.
Organic acquisitions the last to fail, 121.
Organic consciousness, 108.
Organic memory, 10; how acquired, 14; instances of, 17; seat of, 16; relation of, to consciousness, 63, 64, last to fail, 95.
Opium, 199.

Paget, Sir James, 196.
Paralysis, general, 116, 143.
Partial amnesia, 116; of signs, 151.
Partial disorders of memory, 70.
Partial excitation of memory, cases of, 179.
Perfect memory, 10.
Periodical amnesia, 71, 98; case of, 99, 101, 102, 103; disruption of memory imperfect in, 104; general characteristics of, 105; only a secondary phenomenon, 112; results from drunkenness, 115.
Personality, 98, 107; its true basis, 109; disintegration of, 121.
Physiological cause of amnesia, 96.
Pick, Dr. Arnold, 188.
Present time, 49.
Primitive acquisitions, why stable, 129.
Primitive automatic movements, how acquired, 15.
Progressive amnesia, 116; recovery from, rare, 122.
Pronominal or demonstrative roots, 169.

Pronouns, memory of, 168.
Proper names, loss of recollection of, 166.
Proper nouns changed to common, 169.
Pseudo-memory, 186; explanation of, 189.
Psychical element of memory, 10.
Psychical memory, 17, 202.
Psychology, results of its further study, 79; its relation to signs, 151.
Psychology, the new; its teachings regarding memory, 9.
Psychological importance of movements, 154.
Psychological interpretation of epileptic amnesia, 73.
Puberty, 111.

Quality, notions of, 167.

Recollection, 10; first condition of, 12; what it is, 46; stages of, 55; contraction of, 59; its most unstable form, 62.
Re-education, instances of, 82–94; nature of, 97.
Reference points, 50; what are they? 51, 52.
Reflex action, 35.
Regression, law of, 122.
Reproduction of cells, 67.
Residua, motor, 155; disappearance of, 185.
Residuum, 196.
Rogers, 56.
Roots, verbal and pronominal, 169.
Rush, Dr., 182.

Sander, 186.
Scandella, Dr., 182.
Scott, Walter, 55.
Secondary automatic actions, 14; as shown in locomotion, 21; their relation to consciousness, 33.
Sharpey, 97.
Signs, amnesia of, 151.
Somnambulism, 104, 114.
Somnolence, followed by amnesia, case of, 84.
Stability of recollections, how attained, 62, 63.
Stewart, Dugald, 47, 136.
Stimulants, action of, upon memory, 199.
Substantives, memory of, 166, 168.
Suicide, in epileptic mania, 73.
Suspended animation, followed by amnesia, case of, 82.

Taine, 47, 169.
Temporary amnesia, 71; of a destructive character, 79.
Thought, speed of, 34.
Trousseau, 157, 164, 169, 170.

Unconscious cerebration, 37.
Unconsciousness, 36.

Verbal roots, 169.
Verbs, memory of, 167.
Vernet, Horace, 137.
Vertigo, epileptic, 71; instances of, 72; suicide in, 73; instance of, 18.
Vierordt's experiment on the duration of small intervals, 59.
Villiers, 95.
Visual perception, what it implies, 42; mechanism of, 46; illusion of, 61.

Whitney, Professor, 169.
Wigan, 186.
Winslow Forbes, 45, 56, 97, 183.

FLORIDA FOR TOURISTS, INVALIDS, AND SETTLERS: Containing Practical Information regarding Climate, Soil, and Productions; Cities, Towns, and People; Scenery and Resorts; the Culture of the Orange and other Tropical Fruits; Farming and Gardening; Sports; Routes of Travel, etc., etc. By GEORGE M. BARBOUR. With Map and numerous Illustrations. 12mo, cloth. Price, $1.50.

This is the most comprehensive and authentic book on Florida that has been published. The following TESTIMONIAL is proof of its value and trustworthiness:

"It is known to the undersigned that the author, Mr. George M. Barbour, has traveled almost the whole of Florida, under circumstances peculiarly advantageous for enabling him to acquaint himself with the varied resources of the State, and with the attractions which it offers to the three classes to whom his work is addressed—Tourists, Invalids, and Settlers. Our knowledge of his abilities as a writer on Florida subjects, and of the opportunities he has enjoyed in preparing his book, are such that we can commend it as at once trustworthy and comprehensive—greatly superior in these respects to anything hitherto published descriptive of the entire State and its soil and productions.

"W. D. BLOXHAM, Governor of Florida; GEORGE F. DREW, ex-Governor of Florida; SETH FRENCH, ex-Commissioner of Immigration; SAMUEL FAIRBANKS, Assistant Commissioner of Immigration."

IN THE BRUSH; Or, Old-Time Social, Political, and Religious Life in the Southwest. By Rev. HAMILTON W. PIERSON, D. D., ex-President of Cumberland College, Kentucky. With Illustrations by W. L. SHEPPARD. 12mo, cloth. Price, $1.50.

"Many years ago Dr. Pierson was active in the Southwest in the cause of education and Bible-distribution, and he has here, under the title of 'In the Brush; or, Old-Time Social, Political, and Religious Life in the Southwest,' preserved some of the most salient and memorable of his experiences. The book smacks of the soil, and of a state of things most unique and interesting, yet now rapidly fading from memory and reminiscence. . . . Its vivid, lively, and withal most truthful descriptions of a state of society now passed away for ever, will be read with interest."—*New York Evangelist.*

THE BLOODY CHASM. A Novel. By J. W. DE FOREST, author of "The Wetherel Affair," "Overland," etc. 16mo, cloth. Price, $1.00.

"At last, it seems, we have the 'American novel, with letters royal to attest its birthright. The author has well chosen his time, just when 'the war of secession was ended.' The persons he brings forward are real people, our own people; we know them. They are never overdrawn, but most intensely alive they are with the passions and prejudices of those times. The heroine is a South Carolinian—Mr. De Forest does not exaggerate in his pictures of her bravery in facing poverty, her audacity of speech, and the bitterness of her sectional hatred. He always keeps on the tip of his pencil, though, a certain leaven of honey that makes us love her and cry 'Bravo!' to her inconsistencies. There are other characters in the book, notably that of Aunt Chloe, the delineation of which has never been surpassed. . . .

"The story seems well adapted to dramatization, it is so full of incident, so alive with striking situations, varied characters, pithy and vivacious dialogue."

The scene opens in Charleston soon after the war, and the story turns, as the title implies, upon the sectional passions pertaining to the struggle, which were then at their height.

For sale by all booksellers; or sent by mail, post-paid, on receipt of price.

New York: D. APPLETON & CO., 1, 3, & 5 Bond Street.